S0-ABD-577

LITERATURE SALES ORDER FORM

NAME: _____

COMPANY: _____

ADDRESS: _____

CITY: _____ STATE: _____ ZIP: _____

COUNTRY: _____

PHONE NO.: (_____) _____

ORDER NO.	TITLE	QTY.		PRICE		TOTAL
☐☐☐☐☐☐	_____	_____	×	_____	=	_____
☐☐☐☐☐☐	_____	_____	×	_____	=	_____
☐☐☐☐☐☐	_____	_____	×	_____	=	_____
☐☐☐☐☐☐	_____	_____	×	_____	=	_____
☐☐☐☐☐☐	_____	_____	×	_____	=	_____
☐☐☐☐☐☐	_____	_____	×	_____	=	_____
☐☐☐☐☐☐	_____	_____	×	_____	=	_____
☐☐☐☐☐☐	_____	_____	×	_____	=	_____
☐☐☐☐☐☐	_____	_____	×	_____	=	_____
☐☐☐☐☐☐	_____	_____	×	_____	=	_____

Subtotal _____

Must Add Your
Local Sales Tax _____

Must add appropriate postage to subtotal
(10% U.S. and Canada, 20% all other) ⟶ Postage _____

Total _____

Pay by Visa, MasterCard, American Express, Check, Money Order, or company purchase order payable to Intel Literature Sales. Allow 2-4 weeks for delivery.

☐ Visa ☐ MasterCard ☐ American Express Expiration Date _____

Account No. _____

Signature: _____

Mail To: Intel Literature Sales
P.O. Box 58130
Santa Clara, CA
95052-8130

International Customers outside the U.S. and Canada should contact their local Intel Sales Office or Distributor listed in the back of most Intel literature.
European Literature Order Form in back of book.

Call Toll Free: **(800) 548-4725** for phone orders

Prices good until 12/31/88.

Source HB

Mail To: Intel Literature Sales
P.O. Box 58130
Santa Clara, CA 95052-8130

CUSTOMER SUPPORT

CUSTOMER SUPPORT

Customer Support is Intel's complete support service that provides Intel customers with hardware support, software support, customer training, and consulting services. For more information contact your local sales offices.

After a customer purchases any system hardware or software product, service and support become major factors in determining whether that product will continue to meet a customer's expectations. Such support requires an international support organization and a breadth of programs to meet a variety of customer needs. As you might expect, Intel's customer support is quite extensive. It includes factory repair services and worldwide field service offices providing hardware repair services, software support services, customer training classes, and consulting services.

HARDWARE SUPPORT SERVICES

Intel is committed to providing an international service support package through a wide variety of service offerings available from Intel Hardware Support.

SOFTWARE SUPPORT SERVICES

Intel's software support consists of two levels of contracts. Standard support includes TIPS (Technical Information Phone Service), updates and subscription service (product-specific troubleshooting guides and COMMENTS Magazine). Basic support includes updates and the subscription service. Contracts are sold in environments which represent product groupings (i.e., iRMX environment).

CONSULTING SERVICES

Intel provides field systems engineering services for any phase of your development or support effort. You can use our systems engineers in a variety of ways ranging from assistance in using a new product, developing an application, personalizing training, and customizing or tailoring an Intel product to providing technical and management consulting. Systems Engineers are well versed in technical areas such as microcommunications, real-time applications, embedded microcontrollers, and network services. You know your application needs; we know our products. Working together we can help you get a successful product to market in the least possible time.

CUSTOMER TRAINING

Intel offers a wide range of instructional programs covering various aspects of system design and implementation. In just three to ten days a limited number of individuals learn more in a single workshop than in weeks of self-study. For optimum convenience, workshops are scheduled regularly at Training Centers worldwide or we can take our workshops to you for on-site instruction. Covering a wide variety of topics, Intel's major course categories include: architecture and assembly language, programming and operating systems, bitbus and LAN applications.

80386
SYSTEM SOFTWARE
WRITER'S GUIDE

1987

Intel Corporation makes no warranty for the use of its products and assumes no responsibility for any errors which may appear in this document nor does it make a commitment to update the information contained herein.

Intel retains the right to make changes to these specifications at any time, without notice.

Contact your local sales office to obtain the latest specifications before placing your order.

The following are trademarks of Intel Corporation and may only be used to identify Intel Products:

Above, BITBUS, COMMputer, CREDIT, Data Pipeline, FASTPATH, Genius, i, î, ICE, iCEL, iCS, iDBP, iDIS, I²ICE, iLBX, i_m, iMDDX, iMMX, Inboard, Insite, Intel, intel, intelBOS, Intel Certified, Intelevision, inteligent Identifier, inteligent Programming, Intellec, Intellink, iOSP, iPDS, iPSC, iRMK, iRMX, iSBC, iSBX, iSDM, iSXM, KEPROM, Library Manager, MAPNET, MCS, Megachassis, MICROMAINFRAME, MULTIBUS, MULTICHANNEL, MULTIMODULE, MultiSERVER, ONCE, OpenNET, OTP, PC BUBBLE, Plug-A-Bubble, PROMPT, Promware, QUEST, QueX, Quick-Pulse Programming, Ripplemode, RMX/80, RUPI, Seamless, SLD, SugarCube, SupportNET, UPI, and VLSiCEL, and the combination of ICE, iCS, iRMX, iSBC, iSBX, iSXM, MCS, or UPI and a numerical suffix, 4-SITE.

MDS is an ordering code only and is not used as a product name or trademark. MDS® is a registered trademark of Mohawk Data Sciences Corporation.

*MULTIBUS is a patented Intel bus.

Additional copies of this manual or other Intel literature may be obtained from:

Intel Corporation
Literature Sales
P.O. Box 58130
Santa Clara, CA 95052-8130

CG-1/18/88

PREFACE

The *80386 System Software Writer's Guide* describes the interface between the 80386 system architecture and low-level operating system mechanisms. It does not discuss operating system policy issues or operating system facilities that are independent of a processor's architecture. For example, the book shows how an operating system can use the 80386's task switch instruction to dispatch a new task (process), but it does not discuss the many policies an operating system could adopt for selecting the task to be dispatched. To cite another example, the *80386 System Software Writer's Guide* covers the 80386's facilities for device input/output, but leaves the discussion of file I/O to operating system textbooks.

AUDIENCE

This book has been written primarily for the systems programmer who is developing an operating system for the 80386 microprocessor. Programmers writing other systems software, such as linkers and utilities, may also benefit from reading this book. The book can also be valuable to anyone who wants to see how 80386 architectural facilities support common operating system mechanisms.

To use this book successfully, you must be thoroughly familiar with multitasking operating systems.

RELATED PUBLICATIONS

The *80386 System Software Writer's Guide* is one of four Intel publications that describe the 80386 microprocessor. The others are

*   *Introduction to the 80386,* Order No. 231252
*   *80386 Programmer's Reference Manual,* Order No. 230985
*   *80386 Hardware Reference Manual,* Order No. 231298

The *80386 System Software Writer's Guide* can be read independently of the *80386 Hardware Reference Manual*. The *Introduction to the 80386* is a prerequisite to this book and the *80386 Programmer's Reference Manual* is a companion to it.

Before reading this book you should thoroughly understand the material in the *Introduction to the 80386,* especially Chapters 2 (Application Architecture) and 3 (System Architecture). If you are interested in running 8086 or 80286 programs on the 80386, you need to read Chapter 4 (Architectural Compatibility) as well. Before reading this book you should browse through the *80386 Programmer's Reference Manual* and you should keep it handy while reading the *80386 System Software Writer's Guide*. The 80386 System Software Writer's Guide frequently simplifies the presentation of architectural features in order to more clearly show how these features relate to operating system mechanisms. When you want the definitive description of any 80386 facility, consult the *80386 Programmer's Reference Manual*.

Some examples in this guide are written in ASM386, Intel's 80386 assembly language, documented in the *ASM386 Assembly Language Reference Manual,* Order No. 122332.

HOW TO READ THIS BOOK

The ten chapters of the *80386 System Software Writer's Guide* are generally arranged so that the most specialized topics are covered at the end of the guide. The first seven chapters describe the 80386's protected 32-bit operation, the mode of operation most likely to be selected for new 80386 applications. Features that make the 80386 compatible with earlier Intel 86 family processors are described in Chapters 8 and 9, while Chapter 10 describes one way to implement the UNIX System V operating system on the 80386.

Chapters 1 and 2 describe tasking and memory management. These topics are very closely related and you will find frequent references in the first chapter to the second. Having read the *Introduction to the 80386,* however, most readers should understand enough about the 80386's memory management facilities to ignore these inevitable forward references. The third chapter covers interrupts and their close relatives, exceptions. Chapter 4 describes how operating system calls can be implemented on the 80386. Chapter 5 describes the 80386's input/output facilities. The first five chapters describe the 80386 as if it were already running in protected 32-bit mode, with all architecture-defined data structures (for example, page tables) in place. Chapter 6 tells you how to take the 80386 from a hardware RESET to protected 32-bit operation.

The last four chapters cover specialized topics and can be read selectively. Chapter 7 describes the interaction between an 80386 operating system and the 80287 and 80387 numerics coprocessors (or their software emulators). Chapters 8 and 9 describe 80386 facilities for running existing 80286 and 8086 software. The final chapter is an extended example that describes one way to implement the UNIX System V operating system on the 80386.

Note that the code examples given in this book have not been tested.

TABLE OF CONTENTS

Figures

Tables

Tasks 1

CHAPTER 1
TASKS

The 80386 is fundamentally a multitasking computer. Although the processor can be used in single task systems, most facilities of its system architecture are designed to support the concurrent execution of multiple tasks. For example, memory management, protection, and exception handling are all task-based. The 80386 can perform a task switch (context switch) upon direction from the operating system or automatically in response to an interrupt or exception. This chapter describes the 80386 facilities that an operating system can use to create and manage tasks; those aspects of tasking that relate to interrupt and exception handling are described in Chapter 3.

1.1 THE TASK EXECUTION ENVIRONMENT

Figure 1-1 shows the architecture-defined registers and data structures that an 80386 task may use during its execution. Most of the data structures shown in Figure 1-1 are more closely related to interrupt handling and memory management than task management and are therefore described in later chapters. The task state segment (TSS), however, is central to task management and is the principal subject of this chapter.

1.2 TASK STATE SEGMENTS AND DESCRIPTORS

The state of a task can be considered in two parts: the *machine state*, consisting mainly of register values, and the *software state*, consisting of file descriptors, scheduling parameters, and other operating system-defined data. A multitasking operating system traditionally records each task's machine state and software state in a "task control block" or a similarly named record (or collection of records).

The 80386 system architecture defines a record that holds the machine state of a task. This record is called a task state segment and is illustrated in Figure 1-2. The operating system initializes the TSS of a new task, but the 80386 maintains the TSS, reading and writing it on task switches and reading it on privilege level changes. The 80386 specifies the format of only the first 26 double words, and, optionally, up to the last 8K bytes (the I/O Bit-map for the 64K I/O address space) of the TSS. An operating system is free to use the area between the I/O Bit-map and the TSS core (first 26 double words) to record a task's software state.

Because a TSS is an 80386-defined segment, it must have a descriptor. Figure 1-3 shows the format of an 80386 TSS descriptor. The base, limit, granularity, available, present, and descriptor privilege level fields are identical to their code and data segment descriptor counterparts (these are described in Chapter 2). Note that the TSS limit must account for the optional I/O permission map and the task software state, if these fields are defined and used by the operating system (the I/O permission map is described in Chapter 5). If no I/O permission map is present, the limit must be set to at least 68H (the length of the machine state data); if the operating system extends a TSS with software state information,

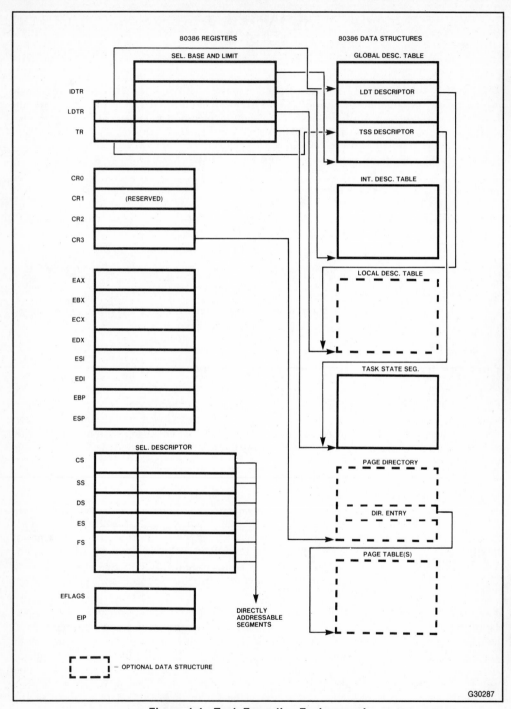

Figure 1-1. Task Execution Environment

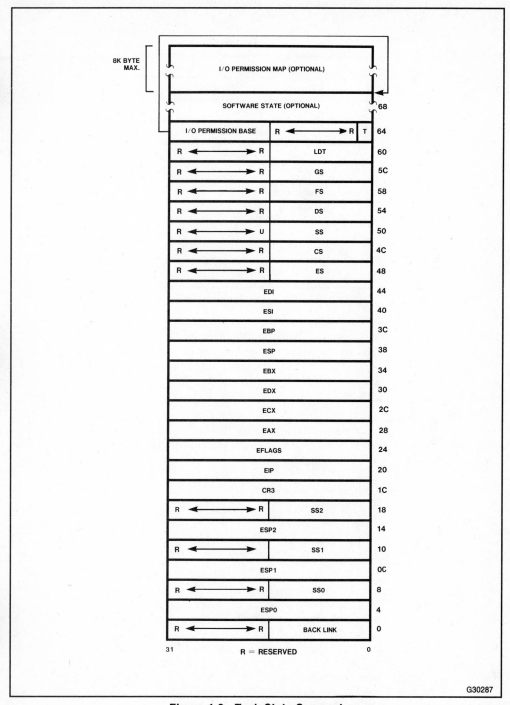

Figure 1-2. Task State Segment

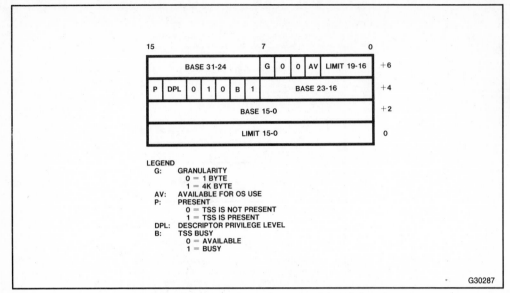

Figure 1-3. Task State Segment Descriptor

the limit can, but need not, cover the additional information. TSSs must reside in the global descriptor table (GDT) to give the processor access to all TSSs regardless of the task that is running (interrupt and exceptions can trigger task switches as described in Chapter 3). To prevent unauthorized task switches, TSS descriptors should be assigned privilege level 0.

The 80386 sets the busy (B) bit in a TSS descriptor to trap an attempt to invoke a task recursively; the operating system should initialize this bit to 0. In a normal task switch, the 80386 sets the busy bit of the new task and clears the busy bit of the old task. However, in a nested task switch, the 80386 leaves the old task's busy bit set. A nested task switch occurs when one task calls another or, more commonly, when the 80386 invokes an interrupt or exception handler that is implemented as a task (see Chapter 3). An attempt to invoke a task whose busy bit is set results in an invalid TSS exception.

1.3 TASK CREATION

The 80386-defined data structures shown in Figure 1-1 must be in place before switching to a new task. The GDT and the interrupt descriptor table (IDT) are system-wide resources, which can be created statically by the Intel System Builder utility, or by the operating system at initialization time, as discussed in Chapter 6. A new local descriptor table (LDT) must be created for a new task unless the new task shares the LDT of another task, or the system does not use LDTs; the criteria for associating tasks and LDTs are described in Chapter 2. If paging is enabled, the task needs a page directory and one or more page tables (alternatively, all tasks can share a single page directory and set of page tables). LDT, page directory, and page table creation are discussed in Chapter 2.

An operating system cannot initialize a TSS or a TSS descriptor by writing directly into the TSS or the GDT, but must use a data segment alias. Aliased segments are segments that overlap one another in the linear address space; they are described further in Chapter 2.

When initializing a TSS, operating systems should observe the following guidelines:

- Backlink: This field should be initialized to 0 to prevent an erroneously set NT (nested task) flag from causing an erroneous task switch. If a task's NT flag is set, the 80386 executes an IRET instruction by switching to the task whose selector is recorded in the backlink field. The 80386 sets the NT bit and updates the backlink field when a task is interrupted or incurs an exception whose handler is a task, or when a task calls another task. A task can set its NT bit with a POPF instruction, but it cannot update its backlink field without access to the operating system's TSS alias. By initializing the backlink to 0, the operating system makes the 80386 raise an invalid TSS fault if the task issues an IRET instruction when NT has been erroneously set.

- Privileged stack pointers: SS0, SS1, SS2, ESP0, ESP1, and ESP2 must contain the initial stack selectors and offsets for privilege levels 0-2 respectively. The operating system must initialize the fields that correspond to the privilege levels it, or other software, uses. For example, if an operating system runs user code at privilege level 3 and operating system code at privilege level 0, it must initialize SS0 and ESP0. When, as the result of a system call, an interrupt, or an exception, the 80386 changes from privilege level 3 to privilege level 0, it switches to a privileged stack by loading the SS segment register with SS0 and ESP register with ESP0.

- CR3: If paging is enabled, the TSS CR3 field must be initialized with the physical address of the task's page directory.

- EIP, EFLAGS, general, and segment registers: Initialize to values the task should have when it begins to run.

- LDT: Initialize with the selector for the task's LDT; this field must be set to zero (null selector) if a task does not use an LDT.

- T bit: By setting this bit, the operating system directs the 80386 to raise a debug trap when the processor switches to this task (see Chapter 3).

- I/O permission map base and optional I/O permission map: These fields can be used to grant a task access to selected I/O ports (see Chapter 5).

1.4 TASK TERMINATION

Task termination is generally a matter of operating system design and is little influenced by the 80386 system architecture. Typically, the termination process is divided between an operating system exit procedure and system reclamation task. Running in the context of the task to be terminated, the privileged exit procedure has direct access to the task's address space and software state. In brief, the exit procedure changes the task's software execution state to terminated, then calls the operating system dispatcher to run the next task. In more detail, the exit procedure disconnects the task from system resources, closing files, removing the task from any semaphores it may be waiting on, and the like. By severing these links, the exit procedure ensures that these resources are usable by other tasks when the task actually disappears. The exit procedure may be able to reclaim some of the task's memory, but at least a small amount of memory (for example, the task's stacks, TSS, and page directory, if paging is enabled) must be left for the reclamation task to reclaim. Finally, the exit procedure calls the dispatcher to switch to another task. The operating system must ensure that the terminated task never runs again because most of its context has been destroyed by the exit procedure.

The reclamation task is a privileged operating system task that can access task-related data structures. The reclamation task may run periodically, scanning TSSs for terminated tasks, or it may run upon receipt of a message from the exit procedure (the message may contain the terminating task's TSS selector). If passed the terminated task's TSS selector, the reclamation task can find the terminated task's TSS descriptor in the GDT. From this descriptor the reclamation task can find the task's TSS, LDT, page directory, and page tables. The reclamation task can free both the memory these structures occupy and the task's TSS descriptor.

1.5 TASK SWITCHING

Deciding when to switch tasks is an operating system policy issue; the 80386 plays no part in such scheduling/dispatching decisions. (However, the 80386 can automatically dispatch task-based interrupt and exception handlers, as discussed in Chapter 3.) Once the operating system has decided to suspend the running task and run another task, the 80386 provides the mechanism to switch the machine context (the operating system must switch the software context).

Most operating systems use an 80386 JMP TSS instruction to direct the 80386 to switch tasks. There are other ways to direct the 80386 to switch tasks, but they are less commonly used. The CALL TSS instruction implements a nested task switch in which return to the calling task is implied; it can be useful for implementing coroutines and for invoking task-based interrupt and exception handlers (see Chapter 3). A JMP TASKGATE instruction also switches tasks. Because task gates can reside in LDTs and can be made accessible to selected privilege levels, this instruction can be used to extend task switching capabilities to selected privilege levels or tasks.

The TSS operand of the JMP TSS instruction is a segmented (selector and offset) pointer to the new task's TSS. Because a TSS is a segment, the 80386 uses only the selector part of the operand and ignores the offset part. JMP TSS is not a privileged instruction, but to execute it without faulting, the running code segment must be at least as privileged as the target TSS. If all TSS descriptors are defined with privilege levels of 0, only tasks running at privilege level 0 can switch tasks with a JMP TSS instruction.

A typical operating system encapsulates the task switching code in a procedure called a dispatcher. Other operating system procedures call the dispatcher when a task switch is, or may be, in order. In general, any operating system procedure that makes the running task unable to proceed, or makes a suspended task ready, calls the dispatcher. The dispatcher changes the software states of the old and new tasks, updates the list of ready tasks, and otherwise prepares for execution to transfer to another task. To switch the 80386 machine state from the old task to the new, the dispatcher issues a JMP TSS instruction, as shown in Figure 1-4.

```
(*save registers*)

EnterCriticalSection;

GetNewTSSPtr;

If NewTSSPtr not = CurrentTSSPtr
        then JMP NewTSSPtr;

(*old task resumed here when it is target
of JMP NewTSSPtr issued by another task*)

LeaveCriticalSection;

(*restore registers*)

Return;
```

Figure 1-4. Example Dispatcher

The JMP TSS instruction saves the task-specific machine state into the current TSS and loads the task-specific machine state from the new TSS. JMP TSS is thus equivalent to many MOV instructions (and a substantial amount of validation; for example, the 80386 ensures that the descriptor named in the JMP TSS instruction is in fact a TSS descriptor). The 80386 executes a JMP TSS essentially as follows (for the definitive description consult the *80386 Programmer's Reference Manual*):

- Save general registers, segment registers, EFLAGS register, and EIP in current TSS.
- Clear old TSS descriptor's busy bit, so the old task can be resumed later.
- Load TR with new TSS selector and descriptor.
- Load general registers, segment registers, EFLAGS register, EIP, LDTR, and CR3 (page directory base address) registers from new TSS.
- Fetch the instruction pointed to by new task's CS:EIP. This is the instruction the task would have executed next when it was last suspended (or it is the first instruction of a newly created task).

An 80386 task switch does not switch the state of a numeric coprocessor because the coprocessor's context may not need to be switched with every task switch. Chapter 7 describes how to write an exception handler that switches the state of a coprocessor when necessary, eliminating the need for the dispatcher to switch it on every task switch.

The 80386 does not save system registers such as CR0, GDTR, and IDTR on a task switch because these registers represent system-wide resources that are shared by all tasks. The processor does not save LDTR or CR3 because these are not normally changed while a task is executing. (If an operating system changes LDTR or CR3, it must update the corresponding fields in the current task's TSS.)

Note that the 80386 does not save CR2, the page fault linear address, in the TSS (the TSS does not include a field for CR2). However, CR2 could contain task-related data if a task switch occurred during the handling of a page fault. Consequently, a page fault handler must save CR2 before allowing a task switch to occur. See Chapter 2 for details of page fault handling.

Before switching to the new task, the 80386 checks the new TSS descriptor and TSS for validity. These checks can raise the following faults:

- Invalid TSS (for example, the target segment is not a TSS)
- Segment fault (for example, the new TSS is not present, or a segment selected by the CS-GS fields of the new TSS is not present)
- Page Fault (for example, all or part of the new TSS is in a not-present page)
- General Protection Fault (for example, the privilege level of the new TSS is less than the current privilege level)

(The preceding is not an exhaustive list of the fault conditions that can be detected in a task switch; consult the *80386 Programmer's Reference Manual* for details.) Although it is possible to recover from many of these faults, prudent operating system designs avoid faults during task switches. A fault that occurs late in a task switch increases interrupt latency by "stretching" the duration of the task switch instruction by the extra operations required to invoke the fault handler.

If, in a task switch, the T bit of the new TSS is set, the 80386 raises a debug exception after switching to the new task but before executing the new task's first instruction. This exception can be used to notify a debugger that a task being debugged is about to run.

Memory Management

CHAPTER 2
MEMORY MANAGEMENT

An 80386 operating system designer can use the 80386 segmentation and paging facilities to implement any commonly used memory model, including "flat," "segmented," "paged," and "segmented paged." Memory can be unprotected, or segments or pages can be protected with attributes such as supervisor or user, or read-only. Segments or pages can permanently reside in physical memory or they can be swapped between memory and disk, to implement virtual memory.

Underlying the 80386's memory management flexibility are two common denominators, descriptor tables and page tables. The content of these tables expresses an operating system's memory model. This chapter shows how to set up and manage these tables.

In the 80386, segmentation and paging are independent of one another and are therefore covered in separate sections of this chapter. (Virtual memory is also covered separately because it is optional, even when paging is enabled.) Nevertheless, an operating system designer must consider segmentation and paging together in order to develop the design that best supports the operating system's needs. The final section of the chapter gives four examples of memory management designs that can be implemented on the 80386; two of these designs use both segmentation and paging.

2.1 SEGMENTATION

The 80386 logical address space is inherently segmented, but an operating system designer has great freedom in defining the segments. For example, in one operating system the logical address space might consist of a single segment that spans the entire 4-gigabyte linear address space. Another operating system might separate system from user by placing their code and data in different segments. A third operating system might map a task's private data to one segment and data shared by tasks to another segment. Thus, while every 80386 operating system uses segments, each operating system defines them to support its own protection and performance needs.

Two attributes give 80386 segments their flexibility:

- They can be as large as 4 gigabytes.

- They can overlap one another in the linear address space.

Operating systems that use segmentation actively can define many small segments, mapping them to distinct linear address ranges. Operating systems that are not segment-oriented can define a few large overlapping segments; in the extreme case (all segments fully overlap one another), segmentation is effectively nullified.

2.1.1 Required Segments

Although a task in a segment-oriented operating system can have dozens, hundreds, or thousands of segments, even an operating system that defines a "flat" (effectively unsegmented) logical address space must provide each task with a minimal complement of segments. Every task must have a code segment (represented by the selector in CS) and a data segment (selector in DS). A task can have a separate stack segment or can use its data segment for a stack (the selector in SS defines the current stack segment). An extra segment is not required, but the string instructions assume a valid selector in ES. Loading the same selector into DS and ES makes string moves operate within the same segment. ES can be loaded whenever DS is loaded, or just before executing a string instruction.

The F and G data segments (represented by the selectors in FS and GS) are not required. In systems that define multiple data segments, compilers may be able to improve performance by maintaining frequently used data selectors in FS and GS, thereby reducing the number of times DS must be reloaded to make a segment addressable. Systems that address all data through DS/ES and SS can initialize FS and GS with null selectors to trap references that use these registers without initializing them. (Null selectors also improve task switch time by eliminating descriptor checking and loading.)

2.1.2 Segmentation Models

Segments allow processor protection to be applied to programmer-defined objects. Segments can be byte-variable in length up to one megabyte; segments from one megabyte to four gigabytes are defined in units of 4 Kbytes. An operating system, with compiler and linker support, can map programming units as small as individual procedures (or functions or subroutines) and data structures (such as arrays and records) to distinct segments. In addition to standard read and write permission checking, the 80386 can check segment accesses for proper type (code versus data), length, and privilege (a segment can be assigned one of four privilege levels). These run-time checks can uncover programming errors, such as bad array indexes and pointers, that cannot be detected at compile-time.

An operating system designer must balance the protection advantages of segments against their application fit, and their performance and storage costs. Some programming languages, for example, have a built-in view of memory that does not map naturally to segmentation. For example, the C language allows a pointer to uniformly address any object in a task's address space whether the object is a function, a constant, or a local variable allocated on the task's stack.

Run-time segment protection checking takes time. The 80386 minimizes the cost of segment protection by checking many segment attributes (such as length) in parallel with logical-to-linear address translation. Other segment protection checks are made only when a segment register is loaded with a new selector as described below:

• Intersegment (far) jumps and calls reload CS with the target segment's selector and descriptor. When the 80386 loads a new selector into a segment register, it checks the associated descriptor for validity. For example, when loading CS, the processor ensures that the target segment is a code segment and is present in memory. Intersegment returns also take longer to execute than returns within the same segment; again, the processor checks the return address's descriptor. Overall, intersegment control transfers take several times as long as intrasegment transfers.

• Intersegment data references take longer when the selector for the new segment must be loaded into a data segment register; the 80386 checks the new segment's descriptor (for example, to ensure that it is a data segment) before loading it. If the new segment is to be the subject of a string instruction, ES must similarly be loaded. (Segment-oriented systems may be able to reduce DS loading by making some data references through ES, FS, and GS.) Overall, intersegment data references are usually more costly than intersegment transfers because they occur more frequently.

A task that uses multiple data segments or distinct data and stack segments must use 48-bit segmented (selector and offset) pointers to unambiguously identify the segment to which a pointer refers. (32-bit offset-only pointers implicitly refer to the segment whose descriptor is currently loaded in DS or SS.) Compared to 32-bit offset-only pointers, segmented pointers consume more storage space (they are pushed as two doublewords) and require an additional bus cycle to transfer to or from memory.

An 80386 operating system can control the amount of time the processor spends checking segments by selecting a model of segmentation. By employing segmentation judiciously, an operating system can strike a protection/performance balance that is consistent with its goals. Some representative models of segmentation are described below (others are possible):

1. The operating system defines one code segment and one data segment; both segments map the entire linear address space. DS, ES, and SS are loaded with the data segment selector. In this model, both code and data references are 32-bit offsets; after initialization, segment registers are never changed. This model provides the equivalent of an unsegmented, and, in the absence of paging, unprotected 4-gigabyte logical address space.

2. Similar to model 1, except that user segments are distinct from operating system segments; operating system segments map the full 4 Gbyte linear space, but user segments map a subset of the linear addresses. Operating system segments have greater privilege than user segments and are therefore protected from user access. This model uses 32-bit code and data pointers, except for system calls. A 48-bit code pointer is required to call an entry point in the operating system's code segment. (The user/supervisor type of protection provided by this model can also be implemented with page, rather than segment, protection.)

3. Similar to model 2, except that data and stack segments map different areas of the linear space. Because the data and stack segments do not overlap in the linear space, this model uses 48-bit data pointers. With separate stack and data segments, the 80386 can detect stack overflows, the stack is protected from bad data references, and the data segment is protected from bad stack references.

4. Same as model 3, except that major data structures are mapped to different data segments. This model uses 48-bit code and data pointers; CS changes on interrupts, exceptions, system calls, and procedure calls; DS, ES, FS, or GS changes to reference a new data structure; ES is changed to match DS before executing a string instruction (unless the instruction is an intersegment string move).

Each of the preceding models trades tighter protection for reduced performance. The actual performance differences between models depends on the frequency of intersegment, procedure calls, and system calls. In systems that tend to be pointer-intensive and procedure-call-intensive (C programs are a good example) it may be wise to choose one of the first segment models listed above. Conversely, systems in which pointer and procedure call performance is not critical, or in which maximum protection is very important, can choose one of the later models.

2.1.3 Defining Segments

Having decided which segmentation model best fits an operating system's performance and protection goals, the operating system designer must express the model in the contents of 80386 descriptor tables. This section provides guidance for setting up and managing these tables.

2.1.3.1 DESCRIPTORS

80386 segments are defined by segment descriptors (see Figure 2-1). A segment's descriptor defines the segment's location (base address and limit) in the linear address space and its protection attributes. The operating system (or the Intel System Builder utility) creates descriptors, but they are mainly interpreted and updated by the processor.

A task's descriptors completely define the linear addresses the 80386 can generate for the task. Any linear address that is not covered by a descriptor is inaccessible to a task because the processor cannot generate such an address. Thus, the distribution of descriptors among tasks, and the linear address ranges these descriptors cover, provides an initial level of control over accessibility to the linear address space. The second level of control over access to the linear space is provided by the protection attributes of a task's descriptors.

2.1.3.2 DESCRIPTOR TABLES

A task's logical address space map is defined by the segment descriptors in two descriptor tables, the global descriptor table (GDT) and the task's local descriptor table (LDT). These descriptor tables are variable in length to a maximum of 64 kilobytes, giving each a maximum capacity of 8,192 descriptors. The GDT holds descriptors that are global to all tasks; the LDT holds descriptors that are local to a single task, or are local to a group of closely related tasks. A task need not have an LDT, and tasks can share an LDT; for example, an operating system might define a "job" as group of tasks that shared a common pool of resources, including the same LDT. The descriptors in a task's LDT and the GDT fully define the linear addresses a task can generate. (Note, however, that the presence of a descriptor in the GDT or a task's LDT does not automatically grant access to a range of linear addresses; the

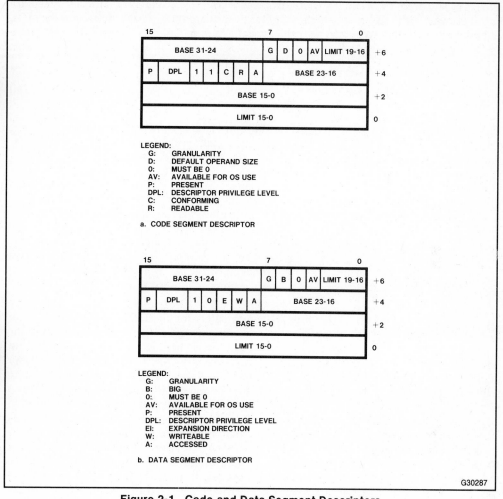

Figure 2-1. Code and Data Segment Descriptors

protection attributes of a descriptor can prevent a task from using the descriptor. Segment protection attributes are discussed in Section 2.1.6.)

The system registers GDTR and LDTR point to the global and local descriptor tables, respectively. GDTR contains the 32-bit linear address of the GDT and a 16-bit limit. At initialization time (see Chapter 6), the operating system loads GDTR with the LGDT instruction. Although GDTR can be reloaded during execution (provided that CPL=0), there is normally no reason to do so. The operating system must load LDTR with a selector for the current LDT; this selector must reference an LDT descriptor in the GDT. If a task does not have an LDT, LDTR can be loaded with a null selector (all 0-bits). The operating system also loads LDTR during initialization, either directly with the LLDT instruction or indirectly by means of a dummy task switch (see Chapter 6). On each task switch, the 80386 reloads LDTR from the new task's TSS. Because GDTR is constant, whereas LDTR (potentially) changes with every task switch, every task can share the segments defined in the GDT and yet have exclusive access to the segments defined in its LDT (if the task does not share its LDT with other tasks).

2.1.4 Aliases

Two descriptors are aliases if they define the same addresses in the linear address space. (Note that one segment alias can frame the linear addresses of multiple segments, potentially even the full 4-gigabyte linear address space.) Aliases can give alternative "views" of a segment to different tasks, or can give one view to the operating system and another to an application program. For example, a code segment is by definition unwriteable; although this attribute prevents an application program from erroneously overwriting its instructions, it also prevents an operating system from legitimately loading the application program's instructions into memory. By aliasing the code segment with a writeable data segment, the operating system can load the application program's instructions into the linear addresses defined by the code segment descriptor. As long as the application program does not have access to the data segment alias, it cannot modify its own code. As discussed in Section 2.1.5, aliases can also be used to share segments between tasks.

An operating system must define a data segment alias for the GDT, the IDT (interrupt descriptor table, described in Chapter 3), and for any 80386-defined segment that the operating system updates. The GDT and the IDT must be aliased because they are not addressable with logical addresses (there are no descriptors for these tables; the processor addresses them through the linear addresses in the GDTR and IDTR registers). Other system segments, such as TSSs and LDTs, must be aliased because of the need to update them upon a task switch or when a task's address space needs to be increased/decreased dynamically. The 80386 raises a general protection exception if software attempts to load their descriptors into data segment registers. The operating system can define one alias for each table or segment described here, or it can define a single alias that spans all of them (or even all of the linear address space). The alias(es) for system tables and system segments should be assigned privilege level 0 so that access to them is restricted to the most privileged level of the operating system (Section 2.1.6 describes privilege level and other segment protection mechanisms).

While they are useful, and even indispensable, segment aliases complicate an operating system. The principal problem presented by aliases is keeping the multiple descriptors consistent. Suppose, for example, an operating system increases the size of a segment. Typically, this means allocating a segment of the new length, copying the content of the old segment to the new segment, and, finally, freeing the old segment. If the old segment has aliases, however, the operating system must find and update the aliases so they point to the new segment rather than the old. Aliases also complicate segment deletion; the memory occupied by a segment cannot be freed until no aliases for the segment exist.

To manage segment aliases, an operating system must effectively extend descriptors with alias information. One way to extend descriptors is to define an alias table that has an entry for each GDT or LDT entry (see Figure 2-2). The alias table entry for a descriptor can

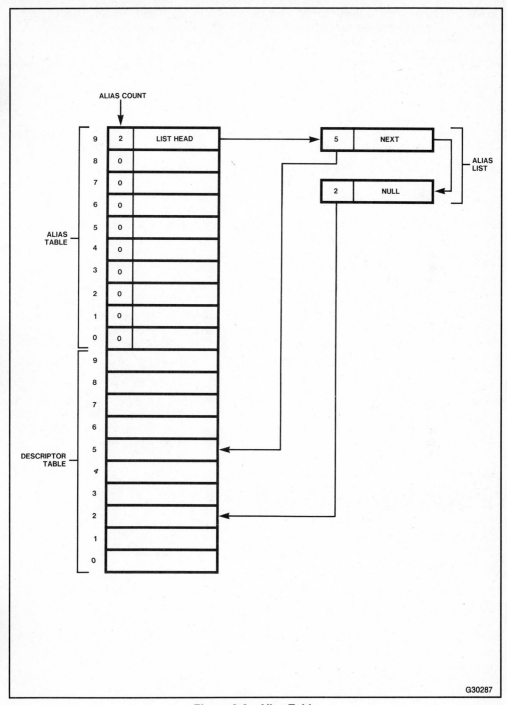

Figure 2-2. Alias Table

G30287

indicate the number of aliases for the segment and can point to a list of pointers to the aliases. The operating system can supply system calls that create and delete aliases; if the operating system makes these calls available to applications, it must check the parameters supplied in each invocation, since aliases can potentially permit access to memory that should not be allowed. (An application should not, for example, be permitted to alias operating system code or data.)

Operating systems that are not segment-oriented can simplify alias management by defining a single data segment alias that spans the entire linear address space. The operating system can then read or write any linear address via this alias and the alias need never be updated.

2.1.5 Sharing

For two (or more) tasks to share a segment, the tasks can either share a common descriptor for the segment, or they can hold aliases to the same segment. There are three ways to effect segment sharing.

*   Because all tasks share all descriptors in the GDT, the simplest way to achieve intertask segment sharing is to place a descriptor in the GDT. Although simple, this approach is nonselective because every task shares the segment. Consequently, GDT slots are normally defined to hold descriptors for system-wide resources, such as the operating system's code and data, that would otherwise have to be duplicated in every task's LDT.

*   Tasks can also share a descriptor by sharing an LDT. Although more selective than GDT-sharing, two tasks that share an LDT share all of their segments.

*   Individual tasks can share individual segments by means of aliases in their LDTs. Aliases are the most precise form of intertask sharing and allow the sharing tasks to be given different views of the shared segment. For example, one task may be able to write a segment, whereas another task's alias for the same segment allows only reading.

2.1.6 Protection

A descriptor's protection fields allow an operating system to define the conditions under which the associated segment can be accessed. If an attempted access violates one of these conditions, the 80386 does not make the access but raises an exception. Exceptions are described in Chapter 3.

2.1.6.1 TYPE AND RIGHTS

The 80386 distinguishes between segments that contain code and segments that contain data; stack segments are data segments. When the code/data bit of a descriptor (bit 43, see Figure 2-1) is set, the 80386 interprets the corresponding segment as a code segment. The 80386 ensures that a data segment is used as a data segment and a code segment is used as a code segment. An attempt to write into a code segment or to transfer control to a data segment raises a general protection fault.

An operating system can restrict the operations a task may perform on a code or data segment by clearing the R (readable) bit of a code segment or the W (writeable) bit of a data segment (see Figure 2-1). When clear, these bits make a code segment unreadable and a data segment unwriteable. Code segments are by definition unwriteable and executable; data segments are by definition readable and unexecutable. A code segment can be further classified as conforming by setting its C (conforming) bit. Conforming code segments are described in Chapter 4. They provide a way to implement procedures that have no inherent privilege level, but execute at the privilege levels of their *callers*.

2.1.6.2 LIMIT

To detect a segment overrun, the 80386 compares the offset part of a logical address to the segment's limit. For example, suppose a task computes an address (an offset within the current code segment) and jumps to that address. If the task erroneously computes the offset as larger than any address in the segment, the 80386 does not perform the jump but raises a general protection exception.

A segment's limit is encoded in its descriptor as a combination of the G (granularity) bit and the concatenation of the limit fields. (In the rest of this section, "limit field" means the concatenation of the limit fields.) The limit field is 20 bits wide; the G bit tells the processor how to expand the limit field to 32 bits. If G=0, the segment's granularity is 1 byte; the 80386 computes the limit of a byte-granular segment by concatenating 12 high-order 0-bits to the limit field. If G=1, the segment's granularity is 4 Kbytes or one page (the term page, as used here, refers to a 4 Kbyte unit of memory and is independent of the 80386 paging facility). The 80386 computes the limit of a page-granular segment by concatenating the limit field to 12 low-order 1-bits. Segments up to 1 megabyte (2^{20} bytes) can be defined with byte granularity; page granularity must be used for larger segments. A segment with page granularity can span the entire linear address space (2^{20} pages = 4 Gbytes). Three examples of segment limit computation follow:

1. If G=1, base=1000H, and the limit field=0H, the descriptor defines a segment with base address 1000H (4096D) and a limit of FFFFH (4095D). The associated segment is one page long and spans the second page frame of the linear address space. Note that the minimum size of a large-grain segment is 4 Kbytes.

2. If G=0, base=1000H, and the limit field=FFFH, the descriptor defines the same 4 Kbyte segment as the previous example.

3. If G=1, base=0, and limit field=FFFFFH, the descriptor defines a segment with base address 0 and limit of FFFFFFFFH. The segment spans the entire 32-bit linear address space.

Byte-granular segments provide precise size checking, but have a limited size range (1 byte-1 megabyte); page-granular segments have a greater range (4 Kbytes-4 Gbytes), but limit checking is coarser. (A reference beyond a data structure allocated in a page-granular segment causes a limit violation only if the end of the data structure coincides with end of the segment.) To prevent unintentional segment overlap, an operating system should allocate page-granular segments on 4 Kbyte linear address boundaries.

2.1.6.3 EXPAND-DOWN SEGMENTS

The preceding description of the segment limit computation holds for expand-up segments, that is, segments whose E (expansion direction) bit is 0. The great majority of segments are expand-up segments. The 80386 provides expand-down data segments for operating systems that meet both of the following criteria:

• Stacks are defined as distinct segments (DS and SS contain different selectors).

• A stack is expanded by copying it to a larger segment (rather than by adding present pages to its segment).

Designers who do not plan to implement stacks in this way need not define expand-down segments and can skip the remainder of this section.

Implementing a stack with an expand-down segment preserves intrastack references if the stack is copied to a larger segment (see Figure 2-3). Stacks grow toward lower addresses; therefore, to expand a stack, the stack must be copied to the high end of a larger segment. If a stack in an expand-up segment is copied in this way, the offsets of the items on the stack change; when a stack in an expand-down segment is similarly copied, the offsets of the stack items do not change.

The 80386 provides two kinds of expand-down (E=1) data segments, small and big. A small expand-down segment is denoted by a B (big) bit that is 0; a large expand-down segment is denoted by a B bit that is 1. (The B bit has a second function for stack segments, whether expand-up or expand-down. When loaded into SS, a segment descriptor with B=0 directs the 80386 to use the 16-bit SP register for implicit stack references, such as those made by the PUSH, POP, CALL, and RET instructions. When B=1, the 80386 uses the 32-bit ESP register for the stack pointer.) A small expand-down segment can range from 0 to 64 Kbytes-1 in length; the G bit of a small expand-down segment must be 0. A big expand-down segment can range in size from 4 Kbytes-1 to 4 Gbytes-1, in increments of 4 Kbytes; the G bit of a big expand-down segment should always be 1.

Figure 2-4 summarizes the differences between expand-up and expand-down segments. An expand-up segment's lowest linear address is equal to its base address; its highest linear address (that is, the maximum offset that can be used to form an address in the segment) is a function of the segment's limit and G bit. The highest and lowest linear addresses of expand-down segments are expressed differently. The lowest linear address of an expand-down segment is equal to its base plus the quantity (limit-1), with the computation "wrapping around" at 4 Gbytes if necessary. "4 gigabyte wraparound" means that the processor ignores any overflow into bit 33 of the linear address; the linear address following FFFFFFFFH is 0. The highest address of a small expand-down segment is base+FFFFH; the highest address of a big expand-down segment is base+FFFFFFFFH. In both cases, the computation wraps around at 4 Gbytes if necessary (always true for big expand-down segments).

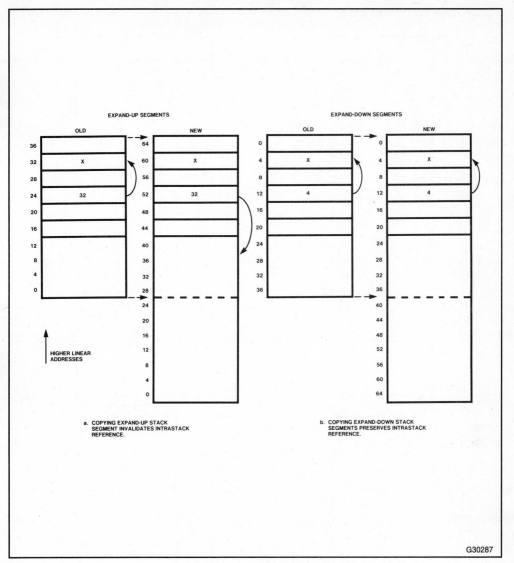

Figure 2-3. Intrastack References

Both small and big expand-down segments can be located anywhere in the linear address space. To define a small expand-down segment, set the base address to (highest address-64 Kbytes); set the limit to 1 greater than the desired segment size. A small expand-down segment can be expanded by reducing its limit if the memory between its lowest address and its base has not been allocated to another segment; otherwise the data in the segment can be copied to a larger segment. To define a large expand-down segment, set its base to (highest address minus 4 Gbytes); set the limit field to 1 greater than the desired size of the segment.

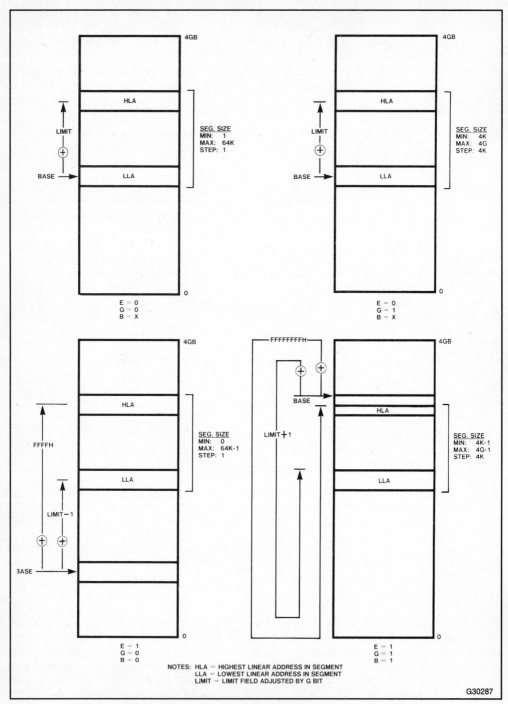

NOTES: HLA = HIGHEST LINEAR ADDRESS IN SEGMENT
LLA = LOWEST LINEAR ADDRESS IN SEGMENT
LIMIT = LIMIT FIELD ADJUSTED BY G BIT

G30287

Figure 2-4. Expand-Up and Expand-Down Segment Comparison

2.1.6.4 PRIVILEGE

The DPL (descriptor privilege level) field defines a segment's privilege level; 0 is the most-privileged level and 3 is the least-privileged level. Unless a task is executing a conforming code segment, its current privilege level is equal to the privilege level of the code segment it is executing. (If the task is executing a conforming code segment, its current privilege is equal to the privilege level of the code segment that called the conforming segment.) When an instruction operand is a selector, the task's current privilege level can be reduced for the execution of that instruction by the RPL (requested privilege level) field in the selector. When RPL is 0, it has no effect on current privilege level. See Chapter 4 for a more detailed description of RPL.

A segment's privilege level defines the privilege required to access the segment. To read or write a data segment, a task must be at least as privileged as the target segment (numerically, the task's current privilege level must be less than or equal to the value coded in the target segment's DPL field). For example, a task running at privilege level 2 can access data segments whose privilege levels are 3 or 2, but cannot access data segments whose privilege levels are 1 or 0. To transfer control to another code segment by a JMP, CALL, RET, or IRET instruction, a task must have the same privilege level as the target segment. For the special cases of system calls, interrupts, and exceptions, in which a task's privilege level is numerically decreased while it executes a more privileged code segment, the 80386 provides special descriptors called gates. Gates are described in Chapters 3 and 4. (The 80386 does not allow a task to call to a less-privileged code segment because such a call implies that a return to a more-privileged segment is also allowed. Such a return mechanism, however, would permit tasks to enter more privileged code segments by returning to them.)

If, as is strongly recommended, the GDT and LDT data segment aliases are defined as privilege level 0 segments, only tasks executing privilege level 0 code segments can create descriptors. (There is no GDT selector and attempting to load an LDT selector into a data segment register results in a general protection exception.) Without the ability to manufacture descriptors, tasks running at privilege levels 3, 2, or 1 can increase their privilege only by transferring through the gates defined by the level 0 operating system.

A task's privilege level defines not only segment accessibility but the instructions the task can execute. Privileged instructions can only be executed by tasks running at privilege level 0. To execute I/O instructions, a task must be at least as privileged as its IOPL (input/output privilege level, a field the operating system sets in the task's TSS); such a task is said to have I/O privilege. However, a task that does not have I/O privilege can be allowed to issue I/O instructions for selected I/O ports; these ports are specified in the I/O permission map in the task's TSS. See Chapter 5 for a more detailed description of IOPL and the I/O permission map.

The four segment privilege levels can be used to implement a variety of privilege hierarchies. To build an unprotected system, every segment can be assigned the same privilege level; the level should be 0 so privileged instructions can be executed. To implement a supervisor/user style of protection, supervisor segments should be assigned privilege level 0, and user segments should be assigned privilege level 3. (Technically, user segments can be assigned privilege levels 1 or 2 provided that page-based protection is not used, but there is no advantage to doing so.)

Privilege levels 1 and 2 can be used to establish protection boundaries within the operating system, or to establish protection boundaries between operating system and end user. For example, a personal computer could implement its operating system at level 0 and assign programs written by end users to level 3. Level 2 might be reserved for third party software, protecting this software from end user errors or tampering.

2.1.7 Other Attributes

Both code and data segment descriptors provide an available bit that the processor does not interpret or update. This bit can be used to mark a segment that is locked in memory, or has an alias, or has another operating system-defined attribute.

The D (default operand size) bit in code segment descriptors should be set to 1 to specify 32-bit operands and offsets; the 0 setting specifies 16-bit operands and offsets and is provided for compatibility with the 80286 (see Chapter 8). The 80386 macro assembler (ASM386) provides 'use16' (D=0) and 'use32' (D=1) directives which allow a programmer to define 80286/80386 compatible segments. The linker/loader uses this information to define 80286/80386 compatible descriptors.

The P (present) and A (accessed) bits are provided mainly for segment-based virtual memory implementations and are described in Section 2.3.1.

2.1.8 Building Descriptors

Figure 2-5 shows one way an operating system can store the content of a descriptor in a simpler format. The record shown in Figure 2-5 coalesces the multiple limit and base fields of a descriptor into single fields that are easier to manipulate. Note that the attributes field is stored with the attribute bits in the same relative locations as they occur in a descriptor; the four 0-bits in the attribute field are placeholders for the upper limit field. Figure 2-6 shows how these fields can be packed into a 64-bit descriptor.

An assembly language sequence that extracts the base address from a descriptor and leaves it in register EAX is shown in Figure 2-7.

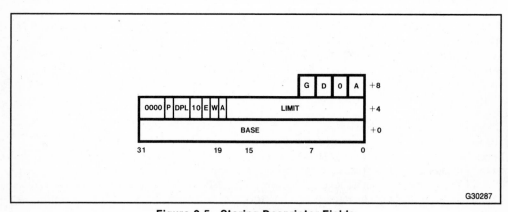

Figure 2-5. Storing Descriptor Fields

```
MOV     BX,Attr          ; Load Attribute word
SHL     EBX,16           ; Chinese puzzle rotate
MOV     EDX,Base         ; Load Base Address
ROL     EDX,16           ; Put high bytes into byte regs
MOV     BL,DH            ; Base 31..24
MOV     BH,DL            ; Base 23..16
ROR     EBX,8            ; Rotate to final alignment
MOV     EAX,Limit        ; Load Limit
MOV     DX,AX            ; Limit 15..0 with Base 15..0
AND     EAX,000F0000H    ; Mask Limit 19..16
OR      EBX,EAX          ; OR into high order word
MOV     Descr,EDX        ; Store low word
MOV     Descr+4,EBX      ; Store high word
```

Figure 2-6. Building a Descriptor

```
MOV     EAX,Descr        ; Load low word
MOV     EDX,Descr+4      ; Load high word
SHRD    EAX,EDX,16       ; Align Base 23..0
AND     EAX,00FFFFFFH    ; Clear AR byte
AND     EDX,0FF000000H   ; Mask Base 31..24
OR      EAX,EDX          ; EAX holds base
```

Figure 2-7. Extracting a Descriptor's Base Address

2.2 PAGING

Every 80386 operating system implements some model of segmentation, but paging is optional. Although paging is typically used to implement virtual memory, its relocation and protection facilities can be used for other uses as well. For example, virtual 86 mode tasks (see Chapter 9) generate addresses that fall into the first megabyte of the linear address space. An operating system that runs multiple virtual 86 mode tasks can use paging to direct their accesses to different pages of the physical address space.

An operating system enables paging (typically during initialization) by setting the PG (paging enabled) bit in the CR0 system register with the privileged MOV CR0 instruction. Chapter 6 provides a more detailed explanation of the procedure for enabling paging. Paging can also be disabled with a MOV CR0 instruction. If an operating system disables paging, it must first ensure that it is executing in linear addresses that are identical to physical addresses, because no linear address translation will be performed after the MOV CR0 instruction is executed.

2.2.1 Relationship of Segments and Pages

The 80386 implements paging "underneath" segmentation by performing page translation and protection checking after segment address translation and protection checking. (The word "after" here means logically after; in reality, the 80386 MMU performs segment and page translation in parallel.) Because the segment checks are performed first, a page-oriented operating system must ensure that segment descriptors allow the page protection checks to occur. For example, every page in a read-only data segment is effectively read-only, because an attempt to write into the segment will fault even if the protection attributes of the underlying pages allow writing.

Depending on its degree of segment-orientation, an operating system can map segments to pages in two ways (see Figure 2-8):

• An operating system that defines a few large segments can compose segments of integral pages. In this type of system, every segment begins on a page boundary and is at least one page long. The page is the unit of memory allocation, protection, and swapping (in a virtual memory system).

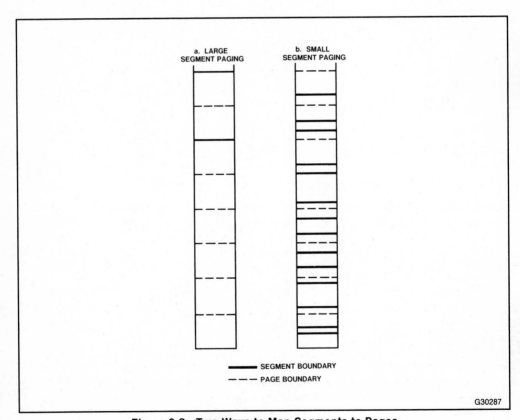

Figure 2-8. Two Ways to Map Segments to Pages

- An operating system that defines hundreds or thousands of segments whose average size is tens or hundreds of bytes would waste substantial space if it aligned segments on 4 Kbyte boundaries. Such a system can, instead, map segments to pages without concern for segment and page boundaries, or it can map related segments to the same page. In this kind of system, the segment is the unit of linear space allocation and of protection; pages are used for virtual memory only.

2.2.2 Page Tables and Page Directories

An 80386 page table defines a collection of 4 kilobyte pages much as an 80386 descriptor table defines a collection of variable-size segments. A page table is an array of PTEs (page table entries); a page table is one page long and must be aligned on a 4 Kbyte linear address. A page table contains 1,024 entries, each of which defines one 4 kilobyte page; therefore, a page table can cover 4 megabytes of the linear and physical address spaces. To prevent unauthorized access, a page table should be defined in a segment whose DPL is 0 or by a PTE whose U/S bit is 0 (the U/S bit is described in Section 2.2.5).

Figure 2-9 shows the format of a PTE. Technically, Figure 2-9 shows the format of a present PTE, one whose P (present) bit is set. The format of not-present PTEs is operating system-defined; because not-present pages are most commonly used by virtual memory systems, they are described in Section 2.3. A (present) page table entry contains addressing, protection, and virtual memory fields; the protection and virtual memory fields are described in

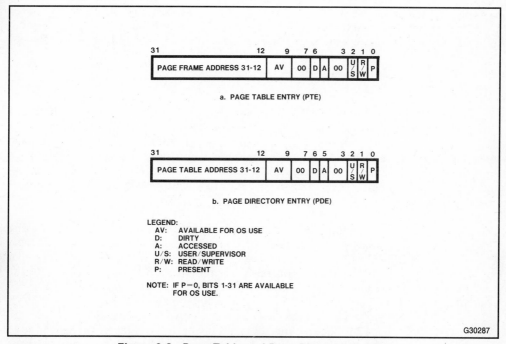

Figure 2-9. Page Table and Page Directory Entries

Sections 2.2.5 and 2.3. The page frame address field of a PTE contains the upper 20 bits of a present page's physical address; the lower 12 bits are assumed to be 0 because pages are aligned on 4 Kbyte boundaries.

The linear addresses an 80386 task can generate are specified in the task's segment descriptors; in the general case, a task can generate any address in the 4 Gbyte linear space. When paging is enabled, the 80386 must look up every linear address in a page table to determine if the address is valid. To translate every possible linear address into a physical address would require 1,024 page tables. Rather than force each task to carry the overhead of a full set of 1,024 page tables (most of whose entries would define not-present pages), the 80386 provides a higher level of page table called a page directory. (Page directories also provide an elegant way to implement page-based sharing, as described in Section 2.2.4.)

A page directory is similar to a page table; a page directory is one page long and must be page-aligned. To prevent unauthorized access, a page directory should be located in a privilege level 0 segment. Whereas each of a page table's 1,024 PTEs defines the attributes of a page, each of a page directory's 1,024 PDEs (page directory entries) defines the attributes of all pages described in a page table. Thus, a page has two set of attributes, one defined by its PTE and one defined by its page table's PDE. Logically speaking, when translating a linear address to a physical address, the 80386 checks the attributes defined in the PDE before it checks the PTE. Should the attributes defined in the PDE cause a fault, the attributes defined in the PTE are irrelevant because the 80386 does not check them. Thus, logically speaking, the 80386 checks segment attributes first, page table attributes second, and page attributes third; any fault detected in an earlier check cancels all subsequent checks. For a page to be considered present, the descriptor of the segment containing the page must be marked present, the page table's PDE must be marked present, and the page's PTE must be marked present. As another example, suppose two linearly adjacent pages in the same segment are covered by entries in the same page table. To make one of them read-only and the other writeable, their common segment descriptor must grant read-write access as must their common PDE. One PTE, however, must grant read-write access, whereas the other specifies read-only access.

Because a PDE defines a set of global attributes that apply to 4 megabytes of the linear space, marking a PDE not-present has the same effect as marking all the entries in a page table not-present, with the added benefit of eliminating the need for the page table. (If page tables are swapped, another PDE bit can be used to distinguish between a not-present page table and a page table that does not exist.) A task that uses 17 megabytes of (linearly contiguous) memory, for example, needs only a page directory and five page tables. The smallest task needs a page directory and one page table.

The CR3 system register contains the *physical address* of the current page directory. During initialization, the operating system can load CR3 with the privileged MOV CR3 instruction. The privileged MOV MEM,CR3 instruction can store CR3. When loading CR3, the 80386 ignores the low 12 bits of the source operand; when storing CR3, the low 12 bits of the destination operand are undefined. CR3 is loaded automatically on a task switch if the CR3 value in the new task's TSS differs from CR3's current value.

To update a PDE or a PTE, an operating system must have page tables that contain the page frame numbers of the page directory and all page tables. Although there are a number of ways to ensure that page frames containing page tables are themselves accessible through page tables, access is most convenient when these page frames can be accessed with linear addresses that are the same in all tasks. Figure 2-10 shows one way to arrange each task's page directory and page tables so they are accessed with the same linear addresses regardless of the task in which the operating system is running. (This example assumes that each task has a different page directory.)

The example dedicates one 4-megabyte range of the linear space to represent the addresses by which a task's page tables and page directory can be addressed. The range must begin at a 4-megabyte boundary, but can otherwise fall anywhere in the linear space, so long as it is the same in each task. A task's page directory is allocated at the top of the block and its page tables are allocated from the bottom; note that the 4-megabyte range can hold 1,024 page tables plus the page directory (which serves double duty as a page table as well in this example). 1,024 page tables are sufficient to cover the entire 4-gigabyte linear space. The page directory is initialized so that each PDE contains the page frame number of a page table, and the topmost PDE contains the page frame number of the page directory.

The 80386 translates any linear address that falls into this 4-megabyte range to the physical address of a page table or the page directory. Table 2-1 gives addressing examples assuming that the page tables occupy the top 4-megabytes of the linear address space. In this table, a linear address is expressed as three components, the first identifying the page directory entry, the second identifying the page table entry, and the third identifying the offset in the page frame. Thus, the first example in the table (1023,0,0) is equivalent to linear address FFC00000H.

2.2.3 Aliases

Two PTEs containing the same page frame address are aliases of one another, as are two PDEs containing the same page table address. Aliases can have different attributes; for example, one PTE may allow reading a page while another allows a page to be both read and written.

Page aliases require the same management techniques as segment aliases. For example, an operating system cannot free a page frame if the page it contains is aliased (to do so would give the aliases access to a page that could be reallocated). Similarly, should a virtual memory system swap an aliased page out to disk, the present bits of all aliases of the page must be cleared.

2.2.4 Sharing

Two (or more) tasks can share all of their pages by sharing the same page directory. This approach is useful in segment-oriented systems that use paging for virtual memory, because such systems use LDTs to separate the local address spaces of tasks. (In fact, such systems typically share a single page directory among all tasks.) Because paging is defined underneath segmentation, two tasks that share a page directory have access only to the addresses defined by the system's GDT and the tasks' LDTs.

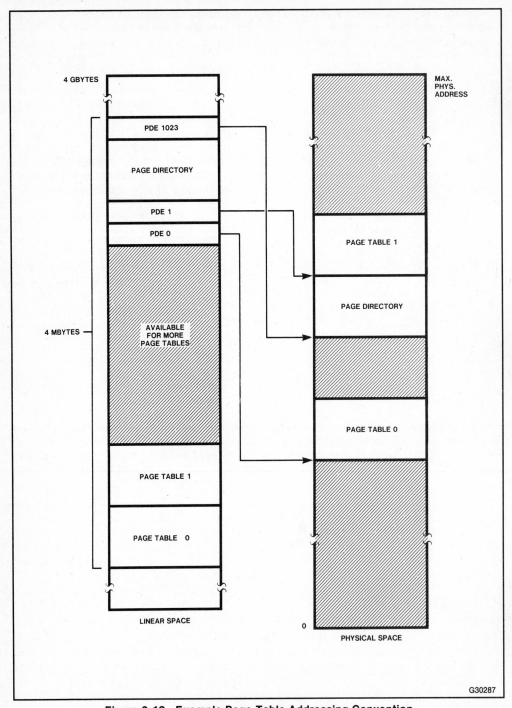

Figure 2-10. Example Page Table Addressing Convention

Table 2-1.   Page Table Addressing Examples

Page Dir Entry	Page Table Entry	Offset	Access
1023	0	0	PT0,PTE0
1023	0	4	PT0,PTE1
1023	1	8	PT1,PTE2
1023	1	12	PT1,PTE3
1023	1023	4092	PD,PDE1023

Tasks with separate page directories can share either page tables or individual pages. Two tasks share a page table if the page table is aliased in their page directories. Two tasks share a page if the page is aliased in their respective page tables.

In general, page attributes are more volatile than page table attributes, making the page table a more attractive unit of sharing. The difference in volatility is especially relevant to virtual memory systems, which change the attributes of a page every time it is swapped in or out. If a page is aliased, all its aliases must be updated when it is swapped in or out. If a page table is aliased, the attributes of the pages it defines can be changed freely because only a single PTE describes each shared page. Only if the attributes of the page table itself are changed do all aliases have to be altered. A virtual memory system can eliminate the problem by not swapping page tables.

2.2.5 Protection Attributes

As mentioned earlier, when paging is enabled, the 80386 logically checks segment protection attributes first and page protection attributes second. Consequently, an operating system that defines pages within segments can use page protection to protect the pages in a segment. An operating system that defines segments within pages should use segment protection, setting the page protection attributes to their most permissive values.

2.2.5.1 PRIVILEGE

The U/S (user/supervisor) bit in a PTE allows a page to be defined as user-accessible (U/S=1) or supervisor-accessible (U/S=0). A task can access a user page (for which it has a descriptor) regardless of the task's current privilege level. To access a supervisor page, a task must be running at privilege level 2, 1, or 0. All the pages in a page table can be made supervisor pages by clearing the U/S bit in the page table's PDE.

2.2.5.2 RIGHTS

Unlike segments, pages are not typed as containing code or data; all pages are executable and readable. However, a user page can be made read-only to a privilege level 3 task by clearing the page's R/W (read-write) bit. Supervisor pages are always writeable by tasks running at supervisor privilege level.

2.2.6 Other Attributes

Each page table entry has three available bits that the 80386 does not interpret or change. An operating system can define these bits for its own use. For example, an operating system can use these bits to mark pages that are locked for I/O, that are to be copied when written, or are aliased.

2.2.7 Translation Lookaside Buffer Considerations

Architecturally (logically), the 80386 translates a linear address by looking up a page directory entry and, using that entry, looking up a page table entry. However, the linear-to-physical translation is accelerated with an onchip translation lookaside buffer (TLB) that holds recently used page directory and page table entries. The processor automatically keeps the most recently referenced PDE-PTE entries in the TLB; it also automatically updates PDE and PTE accessed bits and PTE dirty bits as pages represented in the TLB are read or written. (The dirty bit in a PDE is undefined.) To keep the TLB consistent with PDEs and PTEs, the operating system must flush the TLB when it updates a PDE or PTE that may be represented in the TLB. Flushing the TLB forces the processor to load the updated PDE or PTE into the TLB when the relevant page is next referenced. To the flush TLB, move any value (including the current CR3 value), to CR3.

If the operating system knows a PTE or PDE is not in the TLB, it can update the entry without flushing the TLB. In particular, the operating system can change a not-present PTE to present without flushing the TLB, because not-present PTEs are never in the TLB. To avoid flushing the TLB, the operating system code that clears accessed bits (to identify pages that have not been accessed recently) should be implemented as an operating system task whose page directory is distinct from the page directories of all tasks that have swappable pages. When the operating system switches to this clearing task, the 80386 flushes the TLB because the clearing task's page directory base address (recorded in its TSS) is different from the current value in CR3. The clearing task can then be sure that the PTEs it is examining and updating are not in the TLB because the pages they define are not in the clearing task's physical address space.

A TLB miss can occur on a memory read or a memory write. A read miss occurs when the required entry is not in the TLB. A write miss occurs when the required entry is not in the TLB, or when the entry is there, but its D bit is clear (meaning the 80386 must set the PTE D bit before performing the write). The 80386 responds to all TLB misses in the same way by

•   Asserting the bus LOCK signal and reading the PDE

•   Deasserting the LOCK signal and writing the PDE with a set A bit

•   Asserting the LOCK signal and reading the PTE

- Deasserting the LOCK signal and writing the PTE back with a set A bit and, if the transaction is a write, a set D bit

- Merging the (updated) PDE and PTE into a single TLB entry

- Recording the new TLB entry in an empty TLB slot (if the TLB is not full) or overwriting an existing TLB entry (if the TLB is full)

The processor guarantees that PDE and PTE accessed bits are set before a page is accessed and that PTE dirty bits are set before a page is written. Locking the bus during PDE and PTE updates ensures that, in a shared memory multiprocessor system, another processor does not access the same PTE until 80386's update is complete. (However, the external bus arbitration hardware must implement the actual bus locking when signaled by the 80386; see the *80386 Hardware Reference Manual* for details.) In a multiprocessor system, the operating system software must also lock the bus when it updates a PDE or a PTE. If the PDE or PTE is marked present, the operating system must force other processors to flush their TLBs so they use the updated value when the page associated with the PDE/PTE is next referenced.

TLB misses only slightly increase the overall memory access time of most tasks, because the memory references of most tasks tend to cluster in a few small, slowly changing address ranges. Designers of real-time operating systems should note, however, that TLB misses make memory access times variable because interrupts, exceptions, and task switches can alter the content of the TLB.

2.3 VIRTUAL MEMORY

An 80386 operating system can implement a virtual memory subsystem that swaps either segments or pages. (In this section, the term swap-in means to transfer a segment or page from a swap device—normally a disk—to memory; the term swap-out means to transfer a segment or page from memory to a swap device.) Both approaches have their merits, but page-based systems tend to perform better when segments are large. (Finding a large free block of linear space can substantially increase the time required to swap-in a large segment; a page fits in any available page frame). Because large segments are common in 80386-based systems, page-based virtual memory is the principal topic of this section. For a more complete discussion of segment-based virtual memory, consult the *80286 Operating System Writer's Guide*, Order No. 121960.

2.3.1 Demand Segmentation

80386 segment descriptors (see Figure 2-1) have a P bit that allows the operating system to shuffle segments between physical memory and a swap device. An operating system can use the base and limit fields of a not-present descriptor to store the disk address of a swapped-out segment. However, the other descriptor fields remain defined even when the descriptor is marked not-present; the 80386 checks the present bit *after* it has checked the descriptor's protection attributes. If more space is necessary than the base and limit fields provide, the operating system can define "descriptor extension tables" whose entries contain the additional information for not-present segments.

Whenever the 80386, on its own initiative or in response to an instruction, loads a descriptor register, it checks the descriptor's present bit and raises a segment fault exception if the present bit is clear. Not-present segments can cause several different kinds of faults (see Table 2-2), although they most frequently cause segment faults (for more information on exceptions, consult Chapter 3).

As Table 2-2 shows, a not-present segment can cause the invocation of one of several fault handlers. These fault handlers should call a common procedure to swap-in the not-present segment. The swap-in procedure allocates space for the segment in physical memory, finds the segment on the swap device, reads the segment into memory, and sets the present bit and descriptor's base and limit fields. When the fault handler returns, the 80386 re-executes the instruction that caused the fault.

The present bit helps the operating system swap segments into memory when they are needed; the A (accessed) bit helps the operating system find memory segments to swap-out. When free memory becomes scarce, the operating system must swap-out some segments. The 80386 sets a descriptor's accessed bit whenever the descriptor is loaded into a register. (A segment can be accessed only when its descriptor is loaded into a descriptor register.) When the supply of free memory runs low, a system task (called the swap-out task in this section) can cycle through descriptor tables, examining and clearing their accessed bits as follows. Every-time it "visits" a descriptor, the swap-out task examines the descriptor's accessed bit. If the accessed bit is 1, the swap-out task simply clears the bit; such a segment has been used recently (since the swap-out task's previous visit), and is a good candidate for use in the near future. If, on the other hand, a descriptor's accessed bit is 0, the descriptor has not recently been used and is a good candidate to swap-out. After transferring the segment to disk, the swap-out task can add the memory occupied by the segment to the free pool.

Having identified a segment to swap-out, the swap-out task may be able to free the segment's memory without writing the segment to disk. If a copy of the segment already exists on disk, the swap-out task needs to update the copy only if the segment is "dirty," that is, if the segment has been written since it was last swapped-in. Segment descriptors do not have dirty bits (PTEs do), but their type and rights bits yield similar information. A code segment is by definition unwriteable, as is a data segment whose W (writeable) bit is 0. An unwriteable

Table 2-2. Not-Present Segment Fault Conditions

Exception	Condition
Segment Fault	Loading CS, DS, ES, FS, or GS with a not-present descriptor; loading TR or LDTR with a not-present descriptor (using the LTR or LLDTR instruction); loading CS with a not-present gate descriptor.
Stack Fault	Loading SS with a not-present descriptor.
Invalid TSS Fault	Switching to a TSS that contains a selector for a not-present LDT; switching to a not-present TSS.
Double Fault	Attempting to load CS with a fault handler's not-present code segment descriptor. (This is not a legitimate condition that a fault handler can resolve, but an operating system bug.)

segment need not be written out if a copy of it exists on disk; instead, its memory can simply be freed. A writeable segment must be written out because it may be dirty.

Note that segment aliases complicate demand segment-based virtual memory. When an aliased segment is swapped-out, all the alias descriptors must be updated to indicate that the segment is not present. Likewise, swapping-in a segment requires updating all aliases so they point to the segment's new location. To determine if a segment has been recently accessed, all aliases for the segment must be examined. Because aliases may redefine a segment's type or rights, the need to write out an aliased segment can be determined only by examining all its aliases; one of these aliases may make the segment writeable. For these reasons, it may be simplest to make aliased segments immune from swapping.

2.3.2 Demand Paging

Demand paging essentially consists of two functions, handling page faults by swapping-in pages, and swapping-out pages to free page frames for swapped-in pages.

2.3.2.1 HANDLING PAGE FAULTS

The 80386 raises a page fault (number 14) when, in translating a linear address to a physical address, it encounters a not-present PDE or a not-present PTE. The operating system code that responds to page faults is called the page fault handler. A page fault handler is normally implemented as a privileged procedure that runs in the context of the task that incurs the fault. Because it runs in the faulting task's context, the page fault handler has ready access to the task's page directory and page tables. So it can examine and update the faulting task's page directory and page tables, page fault handler should run at privilege level 0 and should have read and write access to the segment(s) containing the running task's page directory and page tables and to the pages that contain the page tables.

Once invoked, the page fault handler must first determine what the page fault means. The 80386 raises a page fault on a page protection violation in addition to a not-present page. Moreover, many operating systems use the page fault mechanism to signal more conditions than "a page must be swapped-in from disk." For example, a system that gives each task a flat 4-gigabyte logical address space will allocate only the pages a task actually needs, marking typically hundreds of PDEs not-present. A reference to one of these unallocated pages is not an implicit request to swap-in the page, but an error that is cause to terminate the task. To cite another example, operating systems commonly interpret page faults that occur near the top of the stack as requests to add pages to the stack. Thus, an operating system may have different classes of not-present pages. Because the 80386 does not interpret or alter the upper 31 bits of a not-present PDE or PTE, the operating system can encode a page's classification in these bits. However, an operating system should not use the U/S and R/W bits of a not-present page that is swapped-out; if left unchanged, these bits will be properly set when the operating system swaps-in the page.

The 80386 provides diagnostic data to assist the page fault handler. The top of the page fault handler's stack contains the logical address of the instruction that caused the fault and an error code that describes the nature of the fault (see Figure 2-11). System register CR2

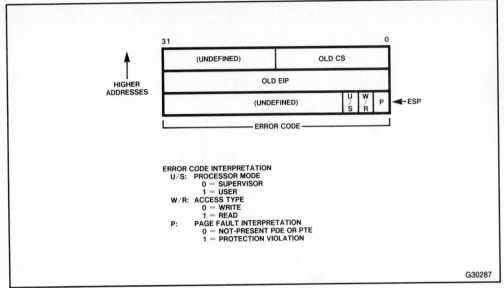

Figure 2-11. Page Fault Handler Stack

contains the linear address that could not be translated; system register CR3 contains the physical address of the task's page directory.

An actual page fault handler must also examine the PDE and the PTE to determine how to respond to the not-present condition. Supposing that the required response is to swap-in the missing page, the page fault handler can proceed as follows:

- Allocate a page frame for the page.

- Find the page's disk address and schedule the page to be read into the page frame; block until the read completes.

- When the read completes, update the PTE, setting the page frame address, marking the page present and not-dirty. (It is not necessary to mark the page accessed; the 80386 sets the accessed bit when it reexecutes the faulting instruction.)

- Return with an IRET instruction so the processor will reexecute the instruction that incurred the page fault.

Page directories can be swapped-out with other task pages subject to the following constraint. Before switching to a TSS, the operating system must ensure that the task's page directory is resident in physical memory and that the CR3 field of the TSS contains the physical address of the page directory.

2.3.2.2 REPLACING PAGES

A page fault handler can swap-in a page only if a free page frame is available to hold it. A swapper complements a page fault handler by swapping out present pages and adding the frames they occupy to a list of free frames. When tasks page against themselves (that is, each task has a limited supply of page frames), the swapper is typically implemented as a procedure. The page fault handler calls the swapper when no free frame is available. In systems that share a pool of page frames among all tasks, the swapper is typically implemented as a system task. The operating system starts the swapper task when the supply of free pages falls below a threshold deemed necessary for good system performance. The swapper suspends itself when it builds the free frame list up to an upper threshold. Whether it is implemented as a procedure or as a task, the swapper attempts to replace pages that are unlikely to be referenced in the near future.

The swapper must have read-write access to page directories and page tables. The A (accessed) and D (dirty) bits in page table entries can help the swapper find pages to replace and to replace them efficiently. (Note that in a code segment descriptor the default operand size and address field is called the D bit, whereas the D bit in a PTE is the dirty bit.) The 80386 sets a PTE's accessed bit whenever a page is read or written. The swapper can monitor page reference activity by periodically testing and clearing accessed bits. If the swapper finds that an accessed bit is clear, the swapper knows the page has not been referenced since its last examination and is a good candidate to swap-out.

The 80386 sets a PTE's D bit whenever the page is written. If the page fault handler clears the D bit whenever it swaps in a page, the D bit tells the swapper whether a page has been updated since it was last swapped-in. If the D bit is clear, and the swapper knows a copy of the page exists on the swap device, the swapper can free the frame without writing out the page.

Note that page aliases complicate the swapper's job. Only by examining all the aliases of a page can the swapper tell whether the page has been recently accessed or is dirty. If page tables, rather than pages, are aliased, swapping is considerably simplified.

2.4 EXAMPLES

This section shows how segmentation and paging can be used to implement representative memory management schemes. Chapter 10 provides an example of a complete operating system, including memory management.

2.4.1 A Flat Memory Design

F/386 is a hypothetical embedded real-time control system in which there is little distinction between operating system code and user code. In F/386, performance is of greatest importance, and protection is of no importance.

To simplify the calculation of worst case execution times, F/386 does not use paging. (When paging is enabled, TLB misses effectively increase memory access times and the number of TLB misses is dependent upon interrupt patterns. Figure 2-12 shows F/386's GDT and linear address space. F/386 defines the minimum number of segments, code and data. All descriptors are defined in the GDT because all tasks share a single logical address space (the LDT selectors in F/386 TSSs are null). Only two segment descriptors, one for code and one for

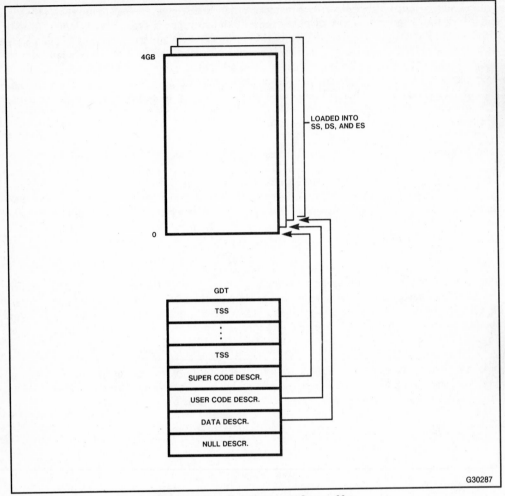

Figure 2-12. F/386 Linear Space Map

data, are required; both have a base address of 0 and a limit equal to the amount of physical memory in the system. Because all segments map the same linear addresses, pointers are simple 32-bit offsets representing displacements from linear address 0 (which is also physical address 0 since paging is not enabled). All segments have a DPL of 0 so that tasks can call OS procedures directly with fast intrasegment calls (task and operating system code are linked together in this simple system).

Figure 2-13 illustrates an actual example of a program running in a flat, 32-bit, protected environment on an 80386 PC. Since the PC BIOS is not written to run reliably in protected mode, this example code uses direct write (rather than using the BIOS screen handling services) to the PC display RAM at the 32-bit address 000b8000h. Note that the code is assembled using an 8086 assembler, and uses the 'db' (define bytes) directive to generate the 80386 specific instructions.

```
8086/87/88/186 MACRO ASSEMBLER X156 ASSEMBLY OF MODULE FLAT
OBJECT MODULE PLACED IN FLAT.OBJ
ASSEMBLER INVOKED BY: ASM86 FLAT.ASM


LOC  OBJ      LINE   SOURCE

                1    ;                Flat Machine Initialization
                2    ;
                3    ; initialization code to turn 386 into 32-bit address/32-bit data flat machine
                4    ; (paging and segmentation features are not used)
                5
                7          name    Flat
                8
                9
               10
0066           11    Data32  equ     66h       ; prefix to toggle 16/32-bit data operand
0067           12    Addr32  equ     67h       ; prefix to toggle 16/32-bit addressing mode
00EA           13    JMPFar  equ     0EAh      ; opcode for JMP intersegment
               14
               15    Tables  segment at 0h
               16
               17            assume cs:Tables
               18
0200           19    GDT:    org     200h
0200           20
0224           21    SetSegs proc    far
0224           22            org     224h
               23    SetSegs endp
               24
- - -          25    Tables  ends
               26
               27
               28
- - -          29    Init    segment
               30
0100           31            org     100h
               32
               33            assume cs:Init,ds:Init,es:Init
               34
```

Figure 2-13. Flat Mode Initialization Code

```
8086/87/88/186 MACRO ASSEMBLER X156 ASSEMBLY OF MODULE FLAT
OBJECT MODULE PLACED IN FLAT.OBJ
ASSEMBLER INVOKED BY: ASM86 FLAT.ASM

LOC  OBJ          LINE  SOURCE

                  35    Start:
0100 B80000       36          mov    ax,seg GDT
0103 8EC0         37          mov    es,ax
                  38    assume es:Tables
                  39
0105 BE000290     40          mov    si,offset NullDesc
0109 BF0002       41          mov    di,offset GDT
010C 890001       42          mov    cx,100h
010F FC           43          cld
0110 F3           44          rep movsw          ; move Global Descriptor Tables to GDT:0
0111 A5
0112 EA24020000   45          jmp    SetSegs
                  46
0200              47          org    200h
                  48    ; Global Descriptor Table
                  49    ; contains three descriptors:
                  50    ; 0h: Null: not used
                  51    ; 8h: Code: code segment starts at 0 and extends for 4 gigabytes
                  52    ; 10h: Data: data segment starts at 0 and extends for 4 gigabytes (overlays code)
                  53
                  54
0200 0000         55    NullDesc dw   0,0,0,0      ; null descriptor - not used
0202 0000
0204 0000
0206 0000
0208 FFFF         57    CodeDesc dw   0FFFFh       ; limit at maximum: (bits 15:0)
020A 00           58             db   0,0,0        ; base at 0: (bits 23:0)
020B 00
020C 00
020D 9F           59             db   10011111b    ; present/priv level 0/code/conforming/readable
020E CF           60             db   11001111b    ; page granular/default 32-bit/limit(bits 19:16)
020F 00           61             db   0            ; base at 0: (bits 31:24)
                  62
```

Figure 2-13. Flat Mode Initialization Code (Cont'd.)

```
8086/87/88/186 MACRO ASSEMBLER X156 ASSEMBLY OF MODULE FLAT
OBJECT MODULE PLACED IN FLAT.OBJ
ASSEMBLER INVOKED BY: ASM86 FLAT.ASM

LOC  OBJ         LINE  SOURCE

0210 FFFF        63    DataDesc dw   0FFFFh      ; limit at maximum: (bits 15:0)
0212 00          64             db   0,0,0       ; base at 0: (bits 23:0)
0213 00
0214 00
0215 93          65             db   10010011b   ; present/priv level 0/data/expand-up/writeable
0216 CF          66             db   11001111b   ; page granular/default 32-bit/limit(bits 19:16)
0217 00          67             db   0           ; base at 0: (bits 31:24)
                 68
                 69    ; Load Pointers for Tables
                 70    ; contains 6-byte pointer information for: LIDT, LGDT
                 71
                 72
                 73                               ; Interrupt Descriptor Table pointer
0218 FF07        74    IDTPtr   dw   7FFh         ; limit at maximum (allows all 256 interrupts)
021A 0000        75             dw   0            ; base at 0: (bits 15:0)
021C 0000        76             dw   0            ; base at 0: (bits 31:16)
                 77
                 78                               ; Global Descriptor Table pointer
021E 1700        79    GDTPtr   dw   17h          ; limit to three 8 byte selectors(null,data,code)
0220 0002        80             dw   offset GDT   ; base at 80000h: (bits 15:0)
0222 0000        81             dw   0h           ; base at 80000h: (bits 31:16)
                 82
                 83
                 84    SetSeg:
                 85    assume cs:Init,ds:nothing,es:nothing
0224 FA          86             cli               ; disable interrupts
                 87                               ; (CLI not needed if immediately after RESET since already clear)
                 88
                 89    ;        lidt, cs:IDTPtr    ; load Interrupt Descriptor Table
0225 2E          90    db 2Eh,0Fh,01h,00011110b
0226 0F
0227 01
0228 1E
```

Figure 2-13. Flat Mode Initialization Code (Cont'd.)

```
8086/87/88/186 MACRO ASSEMBLER X156 ASSEMBLY OF MODULE FLAT
OBJECT MODULE PLACED IN FLAT.OBJ
ASSEMBLER INVOKED BY: ASM86 FLAT.ASM

LOC    OBJ       LINE  SOURCE

0229   1802       91   dw offset IDTPtr
                  92
                  93   ;    lgdt   cs:GDTPtr    ; load Global Descriptor Table
022B   2E         94   db 2Eh,0Fh,01h,00010110b
022C   0F
022D   01
022E   16
022F   1E02       95   dw offset GDTPtr
                  96
                  97   ;    smsw   ax            ; put Machine Status Word in AX
0231   0F         98   db 0Fh,01h,11100000b
0232   01
0233   E0
0234   0C01       99   or     al,1              ; activate Protection Enable bit
                 100   ;    lmsw   ax            ; store Machine Status Word, begin protected mode
0236   0F        101   db 0Fh,01h,11110000b
0237   01
0238   F0
0239   EB0190    102        jmp    Next          ; flush prefetch queue
023C             103
023C             104   Next:
023C   BB1000    105        mov    bx,10h         ; set segment registers to DataDesc(selector=10h)
023F   8ED3      106        mov    ss,bx          ; load SS,DS,ES segment registers with DataDesc
0241   8ED8      107        mov    ds,bx
0243   8EC3      108        mov    es,bx
                 109
0245   66        110        db     Data32         ; 32-bit override prefix
0246   EA        111        db     JMPFar         ; opcode for JMP intersegment
0247   4D02      112        dw offset Note         ; starting address of 32-bit code (low-word)
0249   0000      113        dw     0              ; starting address (high-word of linear address)
024B   0800      114        dw     8h             ; CodeDesc selector=8h
                 115
                 116
```

Figure 2-13. Flat Mode Initialization Code (Cont'd.)

```
8086/87/88/186 MACRO ASSEMBLER X156 ASSEMBLY OF MODULE FLAT
OBJECT MODULE PLACED IN FLAT.OBJ
ASSEMBLER INVOKED BY: ASM86 FLAT.ASM


LOC  OBJ          LINE   SOURCE

                  117    Note:   in    al,61h
                  118            or    al,3
                  119            out   61h,al        ; turn on speaker
                  120
0253 B8330E       121            mov   ax,0E33h
0256 320E         122            mov   ds:Video,ax   ; load EAX with 330E320E
0258 A30080       123                  dw 0E32h      ; Place yellow "32" directly on IBM-CGA display
025D 0800         124                  dw 08h        ; ...by writing EAX to linear address 000B8000h
025D B9FFFF       125            mov   cx,0FFFFh
0260 0400         126                  dw 4          ; set delay count to 0004FFFFh
0262 E2FE         127    Delay:  loop  Delay
0264 B0FE         128            mov   al,0FEh
0266 E664         129            out   64h,al        ; shutdown and reboot
0268 F4           130    Shutdwn:hlt
0269 EBFD         131            jmp short Shutdown
                  132
8000              133    Video   org   8000h
8000 ????         134            dw    ?             ; pseudo pointer to IBM Color/Graphics display
                  135
----              136    Init    ends
                  137    end
                  138    end     Start

ASSEMBLY COMPLETE, NO ERRORS FOUND
```

Figure 2-13. Flat Mode Initialization Code (Cont'd.)

2.4.2 A Paged Memory Design

P/386 is a hypothetical operating system that uses paging for protection and for virtual memory. Figure 2-14 shows P/386's linear address space and GDT. P/386 uses segments in much the same way that F/386 does; however, there are separate code segments for supervisor and user. The descriptors for these segments are identical, except that the supervisor's code descriptor has a privilege level of 0, whereas the user's code descriptor has a privilege level of 3. (The common data descriptor also has a privilege level of 3.) All segments have base addresses of 0 and limits of 4 gigabytes. Because all segments are based at linear address 0, P/386 uses offset-only pointers.

P/386 tasks do not use an LDT because they share a common set of segments. However, as shown in Figure 2-15, each task has a separate page directory. Although tasks generate the same linear addresses, the linear addresses are translated to different physical addresses

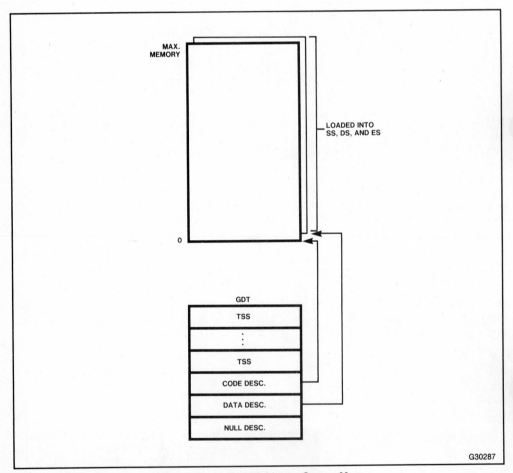

Figure 2-14. P/386 Linear Space Map

(except for operating system references). The unit of intertask sharing in P/386 is the page table; each task's page directory defines the page tables it shares with other tasks. At a minimum, each task has a PDE defining the shared supervisor page table. In this way, the operating system is mapped into the address space of each task.

Although operating system pages are present in each task's address space, the U/S bits of operating system PTEs are 0 to prevent these pages being accessed from privilege level 3. Thus, while an application task running at privilege level 3 uses the same data segment as the operating system, it cannot read or write operating system pages. Similarly, even though a task's level 3 code segment covers the same linear addresses as the operating system's level 0 code segment, the application task cannot directly execute operating system code because the pages containing the operating system's code allow supervisor access only.

The PTEs of user code pages have their R/W bits set to catch programming errors that would overwrite code. (Although the user code segment is unwriteable by definition, it is overlapped by the writeable user data segment, allowing code to be overwritten if it is not page-protected.) User data and stack pages are marked read-write. User code makes a system call through a call gate (see Chapter 4); this call loads CS with the operating system's code segment selector, changing the current privilege level to 0 so the operating system can access its pages. Interrupts and exceptions also load CS so their handlers run at privilege level 0. Segment registers otherwise remain constant.

P/386 shuffles pages between page frames and a pageout device, setting the PTE present bit when a page is brought into memory and clearing the present bit when the page is swapped out.

2.4.3 A Segmented Memory Design

S/386 is a hypothetical system that uses segmentation for run-time protection. S/386 does not implement virtual memory. Figure 2-16 summarizes S/386's memory organization.

In S/386, a job is a collection of related tasks. All tasks in a job share an LDT and, therefore, share all code and data. Tasks in different jobs have different LDTs and share only the segments defined in the GDT (the operating system code and data segments).

In S/386, the segment is the unit of memory allocation. When a task asks for more memory, the system returns a selector for a new segment in the job's LDT. S/386 makes all segments as small as possible and uses byte granularity for segments less than 1 megabyte. S/386 gives a task a small expand-down stack segment. If the task overruns the small stack, the operating system automatically expands the segment (up to a predefined maximum) by allocating a larger segment, copying the stack contents from the old segment to the new, and freeing the old segment's memory. Each segment has the most protective attributes possible; for example, code segments are not readable. No segments are aliased; however,

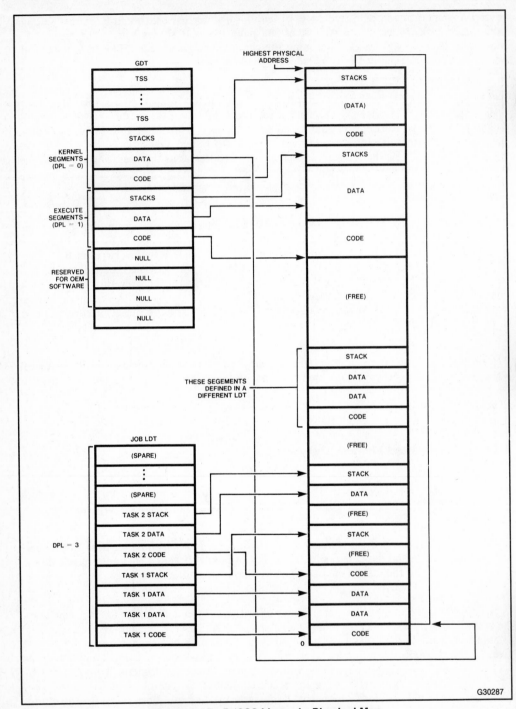

Figure 2-15. P/386 Linear-to-Physical Map

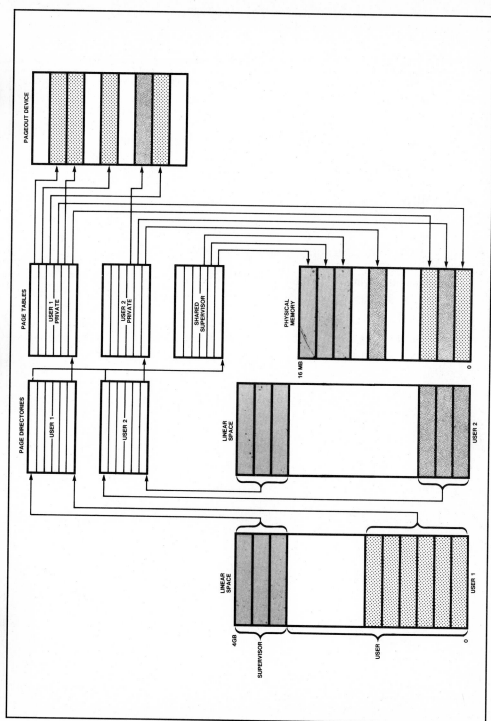

Figure 2-16. S/386 Linear Space Map

the operating system defines a privilege level 0 data segment alias that covers the entire linear address space; the operating system uses this alias to update 80386 system segments and tables and to access arbitrary locations in a task's linear space.

The S/386 operating system is implemented in privilege levels 0 and 1. Level 0 procedures and data comprise the operating system kernel. This kernel essentially provides a system call interface to the 80386 system architecture. The kernel manages the linear address space, created segments, creates TSSs, and so on. Operating system structures such as memory pools and files are implemented at privilege level 1. User code and data runs at privilege level 3. S/386 does not define privilege level 2; an OEM (original equipment manufacturer) can implement its software at this level to obtain protection from user code without jeopardizing the operating system.

S/386 uses call gates (see Chapter 4) to define the privilege levels that can make each system call.

2.4.4 A Hybrid Memory Design

H/386 adds demand paging to S/386. H/386's linear space map is identical to S/386's. Figure 2-17 shows how linear addresses are mapped to physical addresses through one page directory and one set of page tables. Retaining S/386's segment-based protection and sharing, H/386 need not use page attributes to restrict memory addressability because the contents of a task's descriptor tables do that job. Thus, all H/386 tasks share a common page directory and a common set of page tables. The PTEs and PDEs define all pages as user-accessible and writeable.

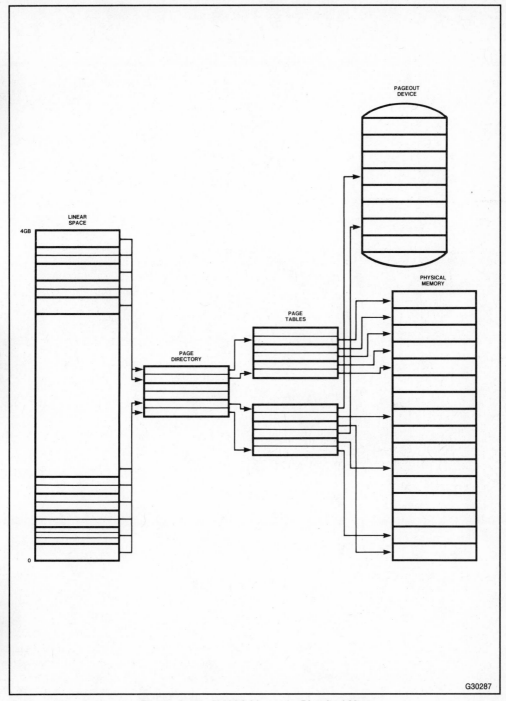

Figure 2-17. H/386 Linear to Physical Map

Interrupts and Exceptions 3

CHAPTER 3
INTERRUPTS AND EXCEPTIONS

Interrupts and exceptions are unprogrammed events that alter the normal sequential flow of execution through a task's instructions. Interrupts occur independent of instruction execution and typically signal requests for service from external devices. The 80386 recognizes interrupts at instruction boundaries, or in the case of string instructions, between repeat steps. Unlike interrupts, exceptions result from instruction execution; for example, the processor raises an exception when it detects an error in an instruction. Note that, by this definition, the result of executing an INT n (software interrupt) instruction is an exception, not an interrupt.

3.1 INTERRUPT DESCRIPTOR TABLE

Each different type of interrupt or exception potentially requires a different type of response. Each type of interrupt and exception has an identifying number in the range 0-255. Some interrupt and exception numbers are predefined by the processor, others are reserved by Intel, but most are available to the operating system. An operating system associates a number with an interrupt source by programming an 8259A Programmable Interrupt Controller; when the interrupt occurs, the interrupt controller passes the number to the 80386. (See the *80386 Hardware Reference Manual* for details.)

The interrupt descriptor table (IDT) is the link between an interrupt or exception number and the handler that operating system has designated to handle that type of interrupt or exception. The processor uses the number as an index into the IDT. The descriptor indexed by the interrupt or exception number contains the information the processor needs to transfer control to the handler.

Like an LDT or the GDT, the IDT is a table of descriptors. The IDT can be located anywhere in the linear address space; the operating system's initialization routine loads the IDT's address into the processor's IDT register (IDTR) with an LIDT instruction. The operating system must guarantee that when an interrupt or exception occurs, the IDT slot corresponding to the interrupt or exception number contains a valid descriptor.

A descriptor in the IDT must be an interrupt gate, a trap gate, or a task gate. Interrupt gates and trap gates contain a selector and an offset for the procedure that is to handle the associated interrupt or exception within the current task. A handler invoked through an interrupt gate is invoked with interrupts disabled; invocation of a handler through a trap gate does not change the interrupt enable flag; interrupt and trap gates are otherwise identical. A task gate contains a selector for a TSS representing the task that is to handle the interrupt or exception. By setting a gate's DPL, the operating system can specify the privilege level required to invoke an interrupt or exception handler with an INT n instruction; to use a gate, a task must be at least as privileged as the gate.

The IDT is a critical resource that should be modified only by privilege level 0 code; this can be ensured by making DPL=0 in the data segment alias that frames the linear addresses occupied by the IDT. To minimize interrupt latency, the IDT should always be present in physical memory. Each IDT gate must be internally consistent when the corresponding interrupt or exception occurs. When updating an IDT gate, the operating system must ensure that the interrupt or exception corresponding to the gate does not occur until the gate has been completely updated. Because IDT changes are normally rare and take very little time, disabling interrupts during updates is the simplest way to ensure IDT gate consistency. Alternatively, the operating system can update a copy of the LDT and issue the LIDT instruction to load the new IDT's address into IDTR; this approach should be used to update the non-maskable interrupt gate unless external hardware can disable nonmaskable interrupts.

3.2 INTERRUPT AND EXCEPTION HANDLERS

An interrupt or exception handler can be implemented as a procedure or as a task; each form has advantages and disadvantages, which are discussed in this section. A procedure-based handler runs in the context of the currently executing task, whereas a task-based handler (which can be dispatched by the processor without operating system intervention), runs in its own context. In either case, when the handler has finished, the processor returns to execute the next instruction in the interrupted task. (For most exceptions, and notably page faults, the "next instruction" is the instruction that incurred the exception.)

3.2.1 Procedures versus Tasks

In general, an exception handler should be implemented as a procedure, so that it can handle an exception in the context of the task that incurs the exception. To resolve an exception, an exception handler often requires access to the running task's address space; for example, the page fault handler must find the page table entry associated with the fault. Therefore, exceptions (including software interrupts) are usually best handled with procedures. (As discussed in Section 3.3, some exceptions, however, must be handled by tasks.)

Interrupts are unrelated to the running task and their handlers are good candidates for implementation as separate tasks. To take care of its associated device, an interrupt handler has no need to access the running task's data, and, in fact, an attempt to do so is probably an error. Therefore, from a logical point of view, interrupts are best handled with tasks that run in their own contexts. When interrupt latency is critical, however, 80386 interrupt handlers can be implemented as procedures. Because most processors have no facility for handling interrupts with tasks, it has been traditional to handle interrupts with procedures. Interrupt tasks, however, have several advantages:

- An interrupt task can run its own address space and not threaten the task it interrupts. (An interrupt procedure bug that corrupts the tasks it runs in is among the most difficult to diagnose.)

- Unlike a procedure, an interrupt task does not need to save and restore registers; the processor-initiated task switch saves and restores all registers. (Automatic register saving removes one source of error from an interrupt handler, but also increases the time required to invoke the handler.)

- An interrupt task can be made to run at any privilege level and, therefore, can be subjected to additional protection constraints. (While an interrupt procedure can theoretically run at any privilege level, practically speaking, its privilege level must be 0. Inerrupt procedure privilege levels are described in more detail later in this chapter.)

- In systems that manage resources on a per-task basis, an interrupt task can issue operating system calls because the task can be given its own resources (for example, a memory pool). An interrupt procedure, on the other hand, inherits the resources of the task it happens to run in. (Consider what can happen if an interrupt procedure allocates memory for a message it sends to a task. First, the interrupted task may not have sufficient memory; second, the interrupt procedure reduces the amount of memory the interrupted task has available for allocation; third, if the interrupted task terminates shortly, the operating system might reclaim the interrupt procedure's message before it is delivered.)

- Interrupt tasks can simplify stack space management. An interrupt procedure inherits the stack of the task it interrupts. Therefore, all interruptible tasks must provide sufficient stack space for the deepest level of interrupt procedure nesting that can occur. Spreading and duplicating interrupt stack space across all tasks, it uses more memory than is necessary and can add to management difficulties (if an interrupt procedure needs more stack, all tasks must be modified). An interrupt task has its own stack.

- An interrupt task may use LDT-based descriptors, freeing up GDT slots, which can be scarce resources in systems with many shared segments. An interrupt procedure must use only GDT-based selectors, because it is generally impossible to predict which tasks it will interrupt, and, therefore, which LDTs it will inherit. (However, if all interruptible tasks share a single LDT, then interrupt procedures can use that LDT.)

Although they have many advantages, 80386 interrupt tasks should not always be favored over interrupt procedures. Many 80386 operating systems will continue to handle interrupts with procedures. For example, when all tasks run in a single environment, as they might in a simple static application, the issues of protection and resource control are irrelevant. In systems where interrupt latency is critical, interrupt procedures may be the best choice; interrupt procedures are invoked faster than interrupt tasks for the same reason that a CALL instruction is faster than a JMP TSS instruction. (For simple interrupt handlers, the complete register save and restore performed in a task switch may be unnecessary.)

3.2.2 Procedure-Based Handlers

To handle an interrupt or exception with a procedure, place an interrupt gate or a trap gate in the corresponding slot in the IDT. These gates are operationally identical except for a single important difference. Invocation through an interrupt gate clears the interrupt enable flag (IF), whereas invocation through a trap gate does not alter this flag. In general, interrupt gates are used for interrupt handlers and trap gates are used for exception handlers. However, some exception handlers, such as the page fault handler, must be invoked with interrupts disabled and should therefore be invoked through interrupt gates.

The processor invokes an interrupt or exception procedure in much the same way that it executes a CALL through a gate. If the gate is an interrupt gate, the processor clears IF; if the gate is a trap gate, IF is not changed. Note that clearing IF only blocks recognition of interrupt requests on the INTR pin; nonmaskable interrupts (on the NMI pin) and exceptions (including software interrupts and coprocessor errors) are unaffected by IF's state. (Note that NMI interrupts are disabled when the the NMI handler is invoked by an interrupt; however, invoking the NMI handler with an INT *n* instruction does not disable NMI interrupts.) The code segment pointed to by the gate must be at least as privileged as the task's current privilege level; otherwise, the 80386 raises a general protection fault. If the code segment pointed to by the gate is more privileged than the interrupted task's current privilege level (CPL), the processor changes to the more privileged stack and pushes the running task's SS and ESP registers. The 80386 pushes the EFLAGS, CS, and EIP in that order (see Figure 3-1). The processor stores the interrupted task's privilege level in the RPL field of the saved CS value. All pushed selector values are 32 bits wide with the high-order 16 bits undefined. For some exceptions the processor also pushes an identifying error code (also a 32-bit value whose high-order 16 bits are undefined).

To return, the handler must pop the error code, if any, and issue a 32-bit IRET instruction. The 80386 inspects the privilege level it saved on the interrupt handler's stack to determine how to clean up the stack before returning to the interrupted task. If the interrupted task was running at the same privilege level as the handler, the 80386 pops the saved CS, EIP,

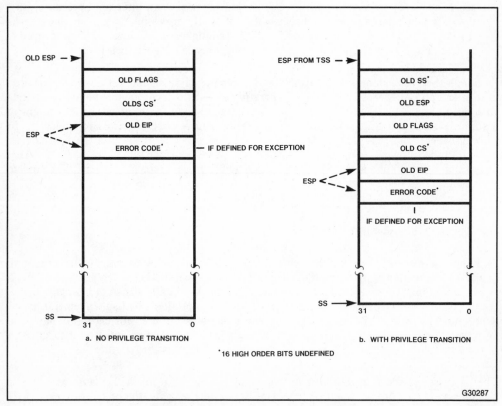

Figure 3-1. Stack at Entry to Interrupt or Exception Procedure

and EFLAGS values into the corresponding registers. If the interrupted task was less-privileged than the interrupt or exception procedure, the 80386 additionally pops the saved ESP and SS values, thus switching back to the less-privileged stack.

In general, an interrupt or exception procedure should run at privilege level 0. An 80386 procedure can never call a less-privileged procedure, and the processor enforces the same rule when it invokes an interrupt or exception procedure. Such a procedure must, therefore, be at least as privileged as the most-privileged procedure executed by the tasks in whose context it may be invoked. In most operating systems, almost every procedure is at times interruptible, including those that run at privilege level 0. Moreover, many operating system procedures can incur exceptions, such as page faults. The DPL of an interrupt or exception handler procedure must be 0 if the handler can be invoked when a task is executing a privilege level 0 procedure. Never make an interrupt or exception procedure less privileged than 0 unless you can guarantee that the procedure will never be invoked when a more privileged procedure is running.

There is a second protection-related reason to make an interrupt procedure run at privilege level 0. When the processor executes the procedure's IRET instruction, it checks to see that the procedure has sufficient privilege to change IF (this can occur when the processor pops the EFLAGS image from the stack into its EFLAGS register). To change the interrupt enable flag, CPL must be (numerically) less than or equal to IOPL. If an interrupt procedure can run in any task whose IOPL is 0, then the DPL of the procedure issuing the IRET must be 0.

A conforming code segment has no inherent privilege level, but runs at the privilege level of the task that invokes it, either by a CALL instruction or by an exception. An exception procedure can be implemented as a conforming segment when the following conditions hold:

- The exception procedure has no data of its own, but operates only on the data of the task incurring the exception.
- No virtual 8086 mode tasks are in the system (virtual 8086 mode is described in Chapter 9). An interrupt or exception handler must run at privilege level 0 to be invoked without fault in a virtual 8086 mode task; a conforming procedure would be invoked at privilege level 3, the level of a virtual 8086 mode task.

Using a conforming segment for an exception procedure minimizes the procedure's privilege level and therefore contributes to system safety and may help uncover bugs. However, the fact that a conforming handler must be able to run successfully at any privilege level limits its utility. For example, a conforming divide exception procedure is appropriate (because the handler needs access only to the running task's data), but a conforming page fault handler is not (because the page fault handler needs access to page tables whose privilege level is most likely 0).

3.2.3 Task-Based Handlers

When, in responding to an interrupt or exception, the 80386 finds that the relevant descriptor in the IDT is a task gate, it switches to the task whose TSS selector is in the gate. This processor-initiated task switch works as an operating system-induced task switch: the processor saves the machine state of the old task in the old task's TSS and loads the machine state of the handler task from the handler's TSS. Note that the handler task runs with interrupts enabled or disabled depending on the IF bit its TSS EFLAGS image. The processor also sets its NT (nested task) bit and writes a selector for the old task's TSS into the backlink field of the handler's TSS. Setting the NT bit directs the 80386 to execute the handler's IRET instruction as a task switch to the task defined by the backlink. Note that a task-based handler cannot be entered recursively as can a procedure-based handler. A task-based handler's busy bit remains set until the task suspends itself with an IRET instruction. An attempt to invoke a busy task results in an invalid TSS fault.

When the handler is ready for the next interrupt or exception, it issues a 32-bit IRET instruction. (Handlers for exceptions that push an error code must pop the error code before issuing the IRET.) In its execution of the IRET, the processor copies the NT bit to an internal register and then clears the NT bit. It then stores the handler's context, including the clear NT bit, in the handler's TSS. Because the NT bit was set at the time of the IRET, the processor uses the backlink field in the handler's TSS to find and load the TSS of the old task, thus resuming its execution. The next occurrence of the associated interrupt or exception resumes execution of the handler at the instruction following the IRET. Thus, a task-based handler runs in an endless cycle; the IRET instruction suspends the task until it is invoked by the next interrupt or exception.

Processor dispatching of interrupt and exception tasks minimizes latency, but it can also conflict with the operating system's task dispatcher. For example, consider what happens if an interrupt or exception task makes a system call. Unless it has been notified that the 80386 has dispatched a new task, the operating system will interpret the call as though issued by the task that was interrupted or incurred the exception. Figure 3-2 shows one way the operating system can integrate the processor's dispatching efforts with its own software dispatching.

An interrupt or exception task's code can be implemented as two procedures, one that handles the interrupt or exception and one that coordinates processor and operating system dispatching. The handler procedure consists of an initialization part that is executed once, and an endless loop that is executed once for each interrupt or exception. The dispatcher interface contains the IRET instruction that causes the 80386 to switch from the handler task back to the task that was running when the interrupt or exception occurred. (When the operating system invokes the handler to allow it to initialize itself, the IRET causes a task switch back to the operating system initialization task.) The instruction following the IRET is the first instruction in the handler task that is executed when an interrupt or exception causes the task to be invoked by the 80386. This and the following instructions can update the operating system's dispatching information so the processor's dispatch of the handler task is consistent with the operating system's information. Then the interface procedure can return to the handler procedure, which can take care of the interrupt or exception. When the interrupt or exception has been handled, the handler procedure calls the interface procedure, which prepares the operating system for the task switch that will occur when the interface procedure's IRET instruction is executed.

To minimize the interval between invocation of the handler task and execution of the first instruction that directly responds to the interrupt or exception, the interface procedure should

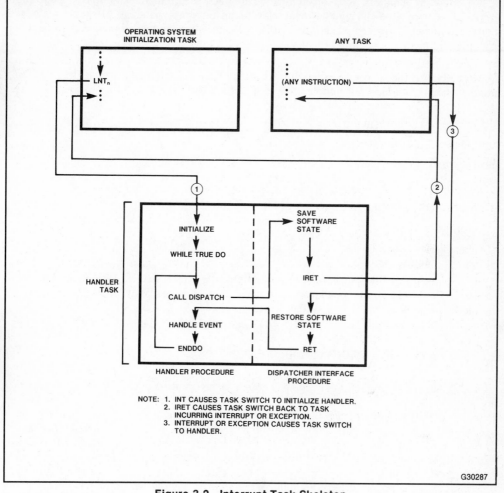

NOTE: 1. INT CAUSES TASK SWITCH TO INITIALIZE HANDLER.
2. IRET CAUSES TASK SWITCH BACK TO TASK INCURRING INTERRUPT OR EXCEPTION.
3. INTERRUPT OR EXCEPTION CAUSES TASK SWITCH TO HANDLER.

G30287

Figure 3-2. Interrupt Task Skeleton

run as quickly as possible. The interface procedure can be implemented as inline code in the handler procedure to avoid CALL/RET overhead.

Some exception tasks may need access to the old task's TSS, or to data in the old task's address space. Such tasks must run at privilege level 0 or call an operating system procedure that provides the data.

3.2.4 Memory Residency

To provide fast, consistent interrupt response, operating systems typically do not swap interrupt handlers but keep them resident in physical memory. This practice can be followed for

80386 interrupt handlers, it is recommended but not required; for example, a page fault exception is permitted during the invocation of an interrupt handler. In such a case, the interrupt handler is invoked when the page fault handler, having loaded the interrupt handler into physical memory, returns.

The handlers for the following exceptions must be in present segments; all but the page fault handler and the double fault handler can reside in not-present pages:

- Divide error fault (number 0)
- Double fault (number 8)
- Invalid TSS fault (number 10)
- Segment fault (number 11)
- Stack fault (number 12)
- General protection fault (number 13)
- Page fault (number 14)

If, in attempting to invoke one of these handlers, the 80386 detects a segment fault, the result is a double fault, except that a segment fault incurred while attempting to invoke the double fault handler results in a system shutdown.

3.3 EXCEPTION HANDLING GUIDELINES

Although hardware protection checking is much faster than software checking, the operating system should sometimes check a descriptor itself rather than rely on the processor. Consider a situation in which a task has asked the operating system to fill a segment with data from an I/O device. Suppose the device driver uses the INS (input string) instruction to transfer the data and locks the segment (see Chapter 5) during the transfer. If the task has asked for more data than will fit in the segment, the 80386 will raise a general protection fault rather than write beyond the segment. This catches the error, but the general protection fault handler may not have enough information to handle the error properly. In this example, "proper handling" might consist of unlocking the segment and returning an error code to the task. Rather than try to prepare the general protection fault handler for every possible condition under which it can be invoked, the operating system can check the segment limit in advance and prevent the fault. The 80386 LSL (load segment limit), LAR (load access rights), VERR (verify for reading), and VERW (verify for writing) instructions can be used to check for protection violations in advance.

An 80386 exception is classified as a fault, a trap, or an abort. An exception's classification determines:

- Whether the offending instruction can be restarted following resolution of the exception-causing condition (faults), or execution can proceed with the instruction following the instruction causing the exception (traps), or the task incurring the exception cannot be restarted (aborts)

- Whether the CS and EIP values pushed onto the stack (or saved in the old TSS) point to the offending instruction (faults), to the next instruction (traps), or do not identify the offending instruction (aborts)

The majority of exceptions are faults; faulting instructions are restartable, and CS and EIP point to the instruction that incurred the fault. If a fault handler is able to correct the condition that caused an instruction to fault, the handler need only pop the error code (if present) from the stack and issue an IRET instruction; the offending instruction will then be reexecuted.

The breakpoint instruction (1-byte INT 3), debug register data breakpoints, and a switch to a task whose T bit is set, cause trap exceptions. (Debug register instruction breakpoints cause faults.) (Do not confuse a trap exception with an IDT trap gate. Most exceptions, including traps, are likely to be invoked through trap gates, but there is no necessary relationship between the type of gate and the type of exception.) Unlike most faults, traps are intentional diversions of the flow of control; CS and EIP point to the next instruction. Thus, a trap handler that issues an IRET without altering the saved CS and EIP values causes control to continue just as if the trap had not occurred.

Aborts are the most serious exceptions; they indicate a hardware failure or an operating system bug. An instruction that aborts cannot be restarted, and the saved CS and EIP values do not identify the offending instruction. Typically, an abort handler can only display debugging information.

The *80386 Programmer's Reference Manual* documents the exact conditions that cause the 80386 to raise each kind of exception. The following sections generally describe the exceptions that are related to operating systems and provide guidelines for handling these exceptions. For the definitive description of all exception-generating conditions and error codes, consult the *80386 Programmer's Reference Manual*.

Figure 3-3 shows the format of the error code the processor pushes onto the exception handler's stack for some exceptions.

3.3.1 Invalid Opcode Fault, Number 6

This exception indicates invalid information (not limited to the opcode) in an instruction. It generally indicates a fatal error in the task, such as an attempt to execute data, and the task should be terminated. No error code is produced for this fault.

3.3.2 Device Not Available Fault, Number 7

This exception indicates that the handler should call the numeric coprocessor emulator, or should switch the coprocessor's context. Refer to Chapter 7 for details. No error code is produced for this fault.

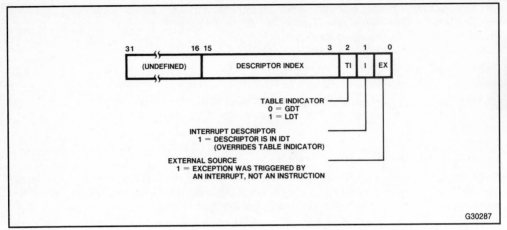

Figure 3-3. Error Code Format

3.3.3 Double Fault, Number 8

If, in the execution of a single instruction, the 80386 detects two faults, it raises the double fault exception. If, for example, a task incurs a page fault and the processor finds the page fault handler is itself not present, the processor raises a double fault. Double faults are fatal to the operating system. A double fault handler typically displays diagnostic information or transfers to a monitor that allows the processor and memory to be examined. A double fault should be handled with a task, not a procedure. An exception handler must have a guaranteed valid context in order to run properly, and the context of the running task cannot be guaranteed when a double fault has occurred. The error code pushed onto the stack contains zero.

Note that the occurrence of an exception during invocation of the double fault handler (a triple fault) causes the processor to shut down without producing diagnostic information. External hardware can detect a shutdown (see the *80386 Hardware Reference Manual*). External hardware can force the 80386 out of the shutdown state by issuing a nonmaskable interrupt or a RESET.

3.3.4 Processor Extension Segment Overrun, Number 9

This exception occurs when an operand of a coprocessor instruction is wrapped around an addressing limit (0ffffh for small segments, 0ffffffffh for big segments, and 0h for expand-down segments). The wrap-around will place the beginning and ending addresses of such an operand at opposite ends of the segment. The operand may span inaccessible addresses if the segment limit is smaller than the addressing limit, and the operand is located close to the segment limit.

The failing numeric instruction is not restartable. The associated instruction and data pointers may be lost; an FSTENV does not return reliable addresses in this case. As with the 80286/80287, the coprocessor segment overrun exception must be handled by executing an

FNINIT instruction. The return address on the stack does not necessarily point to the failing instruction nor to the following instruction.

The coprocessor segment overrun exception can be avoided by never allowing numeric data to start within the last 108 bytes of a segment.

3.3.5 Invalid TSS Fault, Number 10

This fault indicates that a TSS descriptor is invalid or a TSS contains invalid information. This fault must be handled with a task because the processor can detect the fault when it has internally invalidated part of the old task's context, but has not yet completed the transition to the new context. (The handler must run in a known-valid context.) The error code provided for this exception identifies the invalid TSS or the invalid segment referenced by the TSS.

3.3.6 Segment Fault, Number 11

The 80386 raises this fault when it uses a descriptor whose present bit is clear. This fault may be used by operating systems that implement segmented virtual memory (see Chapter 2). Note that a page fault incurred while the processor is invoking the segment fault handler is not a double fault. The processor first invokes the page fault handler; when the page fault handler returns, the processor invokes the segment fault handler. The error code supplied with this fault identifies the offending descriptor.

3.3.7 Stack Fault, Number 12

This fault indicates stack segment underflow or overflow (for example, pushing an item onto a full stack or popping an item from an empty stack) or a not-present stack segment. A stack underflow probably denotes a fatal error, and the task should be terminated. For a stack overflow, the handler can either extend the stack and restart the instruction, or terminate the task. If the stack fault handler is implemented as a level 0 procedure (as is likely to allow quick examination of the running task's context), the handler can run out of stack if it is invoked by a level 0 procedure. The result will be a double fault. Such a situation indicates a serious bug in the operating system, either insufficient level 0 stack space allocated to a task, or one or more level 0 procedures not cleaning up the stack before returning. The error code pushed with this fault contains zero if the problem is with the current stack segment; otherwise, it contains a selector for the invalid stack segment.

3.3.8 General Protection Fault, Number 13

The 80386 raises this fault when a task attempts an operation that is inconsistent with a segment descriptor. Many such conditions exist, including writing to a read-only segment, loading a null selector, and accessing a more privileged segment. Theoretically, instructions that raise this fault are restartable (exceptions are documented in the *80386 Programmer's Reference Manual*). In practice, however, a general protection fault in a protected mode task indicates a serious progam bug and the task should usually be terminated. V86 tasks, on the other hand, can legitimately raise this exception to signal the virtual machine monitor to simulate an instruction (see Chapter 9 for details). Note that if this fault occurs when the processor is invoking an interrupt handler, the interrupted instruction is restartable but the interrupt may be lost. The error code supplied for this fault contains the relevant selector if the fault occurred when loading a segment register or transferring control through a gate; otherwise, the error code contains zero.

3.3.9 Page Fault, Number 14

The 80386 raises this fault on an attempt to reference a not-present page or an attempt to violate a page's access rights. CR2 contains the linear address associated with the page fault; the error code distinguishes between a not-present page and a protection violation. See Chapter 2 for details.

3.3.10 Coprocessor Error Fault, Number 16

When executing a numerics instruction or a WAIT instruction, the 80386 raises this fault to indicate that the execution of the previous numerics instruction by a coprocessor resulted in an exception (for example, underflow). No error code is supplied for this fault. See Chapter 7 for details on the 80386's numerics facilities.

System Calls

4

CHAPTER 4
SYSTEM CALLS

An application task normally transfers control to an 80386 operating system through a call gate or a trap gate. (Other methods—for example, intertask messages—are also possible, but the 80386 provides no special support for them.) An 80386 trap gate is similar to the interrupt vector found in many processors. To call an operating system procedure using a trap gate, a task issues a software interrupt (INT *n*) instruction, the equivalent of the "trap" instruction of some architectures. Trap gates and software interrupts are familiar mechanisms that may be used to enter an 80386 operating system just as they are used in other processors.

Less familiar, but more versatile, are 80386 call gates, the main subject of this chapter. Like a trap gate, a call gate is a protected operating system entry point. An ordinary intersegment CALL instruction transfers control through a call gate to the operating system, automatically copying parameters from the caller's stack to the more privileged operating system stack. Thus, call gates present an operating system interface that is identical to the interface presented by a collection of ordinary procedures. No special measures, on the part of either the application programmer, the compiler, or the linker, are required to make a system call through a call gate.

4.1 CALL GATES

A call gate (see Figure 4-1) can reside in the GDT or in an LDT. A call gate can be defined statically with the Intel System Builder utility, or can be created statically or dynamically by an operating system. If gates are defined statically, applications can name a gate in intersegment CALL instructions, and the linker can resolve the reference as it resolves a reference to a procedure. When used to implement system calls, call gates usually are placed in

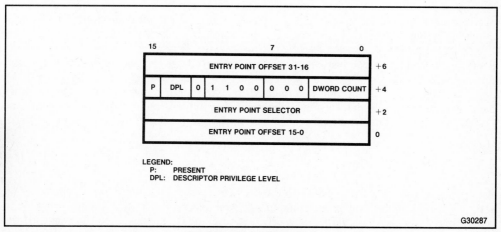

LEGEND:
P: PRESENT
DPL: DESCRIPTOR PRIVILEGE LEVEL

G30287

Figure 4-1. Call Gate

the GDT so they can be shared by all tasks. Placing call gates in LDTs is one way to implement dynamic linking. (The gate can be marked not-present; the segment fault handler can load the code, place the code's address in the gate, mark the gate present, and return.)

A call gate contains a selector and an offset that point to a procedure that is the ultimate target of a CALL instruction directed at the gate. (The CALL instruction itself specifies a selector for the *gate* and an offset that the processor ignores.) Thus, a call gate is the indirect address of a system procedure. As long as the call gate's address (that is, its position in the GDT) remains constant, the address it points to can be changed (as may be required in a new release of the operating system) without relinking existing programs.

Besides providing this basic call redirection facility, a call gate can optionally

- Prevent insufficiently privileged procedures from calling its procedure
- Increase a task's privilege while it executes a procedure called through a gate
- Switch to a different stack for execution of the called procedure
- Copy parameters from the caller's stack to the new stack

It is these optional facilities that make call gates so versatile; they are described in more detail in the following sections. First, however, comes a discussion of the number of gates an operating system should define.

4.1.1 How Many Gates?

The number of call gates an operating system defines in the GDT is a matter of preference. There can be as few as one, there can be one per privilege level transition (that is, from level 3 to level 2, from level 3 to level 1, and so on), or every system call can be given its own gate.

A single call gate that effects a privilege transition from level 3 to level 0 provides the conventional user-to-supervisor transition. This gate funnels all system calls to a single operating system procedure that, in turn, passes them to their ultimate destinations in the operating system.

Providing one call gate per system call can be faster, because there is no intermediate "call forwarding" procedure. One gate per call also supports parameter copying (as will be explained shortly, a call through a gate copies a fixed length parameter list). On the other hand, call gates consume GDT slots, which can be a limited resource in some systems (the GDT can hold 8,192 descriptors).

4.1.2 Controlling Access

An operating system can thus establish the privilege level required to make a system call by setting the DPL field in the corresponding call gate appropriately. Just as the DPL field in a data segment descriptor defines the privilege levels that can reference the segment, the same field in a call gate dictates the privilege required to call through the gate. A gate that is more privileged than a caller is inaccessible to the caller; an attempt to call through such a gate results in a general protection exception.

4.1.3 Switching Privilege Levels and Stacks

Each 80386 task has its own set of stacks, one for each privilege level at which the task may run. (A task needs a stack for each privilege level it actually uses. An operating system that implements a user-supervisor style of protection provides each task with a level 3 stack and a level 0 stack.) The level 3 stack is defined by the initial values of SS and ESP in the task's TSS. The privileged stacks are defined by the SS0-2 and ESP0-2 values in the task's TSS. Providing separate stacks for each privilege level ensures that a called procedure has enough stack to run on—it does not depend on its caller to leave sufficient space.

The intersegment CALL and RET instructions, when used in conjunction with a call gate, detect a change in privilege level and switch to the appropriate stack before executing the first instruction at the new level. The mechanics of switching privilege levels and stacks work as follows. When executing an intersegment CALL whose selector operand references a call gate, the processor compares the caller's CPL with the DPL of the target code segment's descriptor (the call gate contains a selector for the descriptor). Note that the DPL of the call gate controls gate accessibility, whereas the DPL of the target code segment controls the privilege level shift. The three possible results of the CPL:DPL comparison are summarized below:

CPL=DPL   No privilege transition, push CS and EIP on current stack

CPL<DPL   Raise general protection exception

CPL>DPL   Change to more privileged stack

The processor switches to a more privileged stack by loading SS and ESP with the appropriate values from the TSS and by pushing the old SS and ESP values on the stack as shown in Figure 4-2. Note that the caller's privilege level is available in the lower order two bits of the CS selector pushed on the stack after the old SS and ESP. By comparing this saved value with CPL, the RET instruction determines if it is making a privilege level transition and restores the old stack if this is so.

4.1.4 Passing Parameters

Procedures customarily pass parameters to each other by pushing them on the stack and then issuing a CALL instruction. The same familiar approach can be used for system calls that are directed to call gates. When the target of such a call has the same privilege level as the caller, no stack switch occurs, and the called procedure finds the parameters just below (that is, at higher addresses) the return address on the stack (where they would be after any CALL). The parameter copying facility of a call gate places parameters in the same relative location, even if the caller is less privileged and stacks are switched.

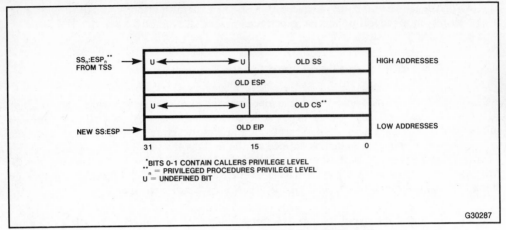

Figure 4-2. Stack at Entry to Privileged Procedure

In each call gate is a field called dword count that specifies the length of the parameter list that the processor should copy from the caller's to the called procedure's stack. 0-31 double-words can be copied. Systems that pass parameters in registers should specify a dword count of 0. If more than 31 doublewords must be passed, a pointer to a record containing the parameters can be passed, or the operating system can obtain them from the caller's stack. Figure 4-3 shows the stack at entry to a more privileged procedure in which the processor has copied three 32-bit parameters from the less-privileged caller's stack. That is, the figure shows how the stack appears at entry to a more-privileged procedure named SysWait-ForMsg after the caller issued the following instructions:

```
PUSH    parm1
PUSH    parm
PUSH    parm3
CALL    SysWaitForMsg
```

Note that the return address and parameters occupy the same positions they would if the caller was the same privilege level as SysWaitForMsg. This means that the called procedure need not be concerned about the level from which it is called. Its parameters are always in the same place whether it is running on the caller's stack or its own. Further, the called procedure can always return by issuing RET n where n is the number of parameter *bytes* that the 80386 should remove from the stack (n should be 12 in the example). The RET n instruction pops the old CS and EIP values and notes (from the caller's privilege level stored in bits 0-1 of the CS selector) whether it is returning to a less-privileged procedure. It then increments ESP by n. Finally, if and only if CPL is changing, the processor pops the old ESP and SS values from the new stack and increments the old ESP by n; the result is a switch to the old stack and removal of the parameters the caller pushed. Thus, regardless of whether the caller calls a procedure of equal or greater privilege, it receives control again with no parameters on its stack. (Note that upon return from a privileged procedure, the ESP and SS values of the privileged procedure have returned to their initial values that are stored in the TSS; that is, the stack is empty. Therefore the processor need not (and does

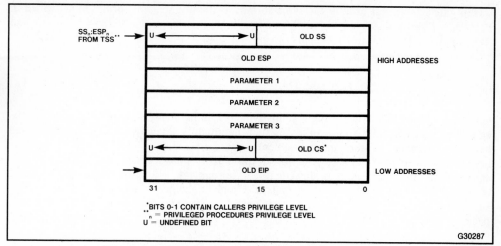

Figure 4-3. Parameters Copied to Privileged Procedure

not) save ESP and SS on the return—they can simply be loaded from the TSS when needed again.)

To return results in a uniform manner, regardless of the level from which it is called, a privileged procedure can use registers or a record for which the caller supplies a pointer parameter.

When using call gates to copy parameters it is best to allocate one call gate per system call. It may be tempting to define a single gate with a word count equal to the longest parameter list needed by any call, but to do so is both wasteful and dangerous. Not only does this cause excessive copying for calls that pass shorter parameter lists, but, more importantly, the RET n instruction corrupts the caller's stack by removing too many bytes from it when the caller pushes fewer than n bytes.

4.2 TRAP GATES

A trap gate is similar to a call gate, and the INT n and IRET instructions are quite similar to CALL and RET instructions. To use a trap gate as a system call mechanism, observe the following:

- A trap gate must be placed in the interrupt descriptor table (IDT).

- A task makes a system call through a trap gate with an INT n instruction where n is the index (32-255) of the trap gate. (Gate positions 0-31 in the IDT are reserved by Intel.)

- Like a call gate, a trap gate switches stacks on privilege level transitions; however, a trap gate has no provision for copying parameters across stacks.

- The processor pushes EFLAGS before pushing the old CS and EIP values.

A trap gate has almost exactly the same format as a call gate; this format is described in the *80386 Programmer's Reference Manual*. Chapter 3 covers the 80386's interrupt and exception handling facilities of which trap gates and INT *n* instructions are components.

4.3 SEGMENTED POINTER VALIDATION

Segment-oriented 80386 operating systems typically define many system call parameters as segmented pointers. The 80386 validates such parameters when system call handlers load them into segment registers and subsequently use them for data references. For example, the processor will not load a selector for an unreadable code segment into a data segment register, nor will it write into an unwriteable data segment. While the checking performed by the 80386 is extensive, operating system designers should be aware of its limits. This section describes two such limitations that operating system designers can surmount with special 80386 instructions.

There is one privilege violation the 80386 cannot directly detect. Suppose a task running at privilege level 3 forges a selector for a level 2 data segment and passes it to an operating system service procedure. If the service procedure runs at privilege level 2, 1, or 0, it can access the level 2 data segment. However, the service procedure should reject the call because the level 3 procedure is attempting to gain indirect access to a more privileged segment via the service procedure. There are two ways to detect such an attempt:

1. If the service procedure has no data of its own, but operates entirely on data passed to it, then the procedure has no inherent privilege level. Instead, it should assume the privilege level of its caller. If the C bit of the service procedure's code segment descriptor is set, the procedure inherits the privilege level of its caller. In the example, the task running at level 3 does not raise its privilege by calling the conforming service procedure; the service procedure running at level 3 incurs a general protection fault when it tries to use the level 2 segment. Utilities, such as numerics libraries, are good candidates for conforming segments.

2. When the service procedure has its own data, it cannot be made conforming because it must be privileged enough to access its own data regardless of the caller's privilege level. In such a case, the service procedure can use the ARPL (adjust requested privilege level) instruction to set the RPL field of a selector to the *caller's* CPL. The 80386 raises a general protection exception when max(RPL,CPL) > DPL of the target segment. Thus, when numerically greater than CPL, RPL reduces a task's privilege level for the duration of the instruction in which the relevant selector is an operand. In the example above, the service procedure's CPL might be 1, but by issuing an ARPL instruction, it can set the RPL of the suspect selector to the caller's privilege level (3 in the example). The service procedure then incurs a general protection fault if it attempts to load the suspect descriptor. Note that simply creating a selector with RPL equal to the privilege level required to use the associated segment is not a reliable method of insuring that tasks do not use more-privilege segments, because tasks can create selectors (with any RPL) at will. Operating systems should validate segmented pointers as soon as such pointers enter the operating system. In addition to ARPL, the VERR (verify read), VERW (verify write), LAR (load access rights), and LSL (load segment limit) instructions are useful for segmented pointer validation.

The 80386 detects many parameter errors, but the time at which it detects them may complicate fault diagnosis and possible recovery. For example, suppose a level 3 procedure passes a bad parameter to a level 2 procedure, that does not use the parameter but passes it on to a level 1 procedure. The level 1 procedure will fault when it uses the selector. The fault handler cannot tell in a case like this whether the error lies in the level 2 procedure or the level 3 procedure. As another example, consider an I/O request that attempts to read or write past the end of a segment. The desirable response to such a request is to dishonor it, returning an explanatory error code. If the I/O request handler defers detection of the error to the 80386, the general protection fault handler will have great difficulty returning an error code to the caller because it does not know the circumstances of the limit violation. By checking the request against the segment limit, the I/O handler can respond properly. Operating system procedures can use the LSL, LAR, VERR, and VERW instructions to check a segment's limit, its type (and other attributes), its readability, and its writeability without faulting. These instructions are not privileged.

4.4 CALLING LESS-PRIVILEGED PROCEDURES

Sometimes an operating system procedure must call a less-privileged procedure. Consider, for example, the UNIX system signal facility. A signal is an indication from the operating system to a task that an exception or an asynchronous event has occurred—for example, that a child process has terminated. A process can declare a signal handler procedure that the operating system calls when the process receives a signal.

An 80386 task running at one privilege level cannot call a less-privileged procedure. (If the 80386 allowed such a call, the less-privileged procedure, could, by manipulating the return address on its stack, return to an arbitrary location in the more-privileged procedure.) An operating system can, however, make such an "outward call" indirectly. To "call" a less-privileged procedure, the operating system can push the desired address onto the stack and then issue an intersegment RET instruction. The less-privileged procedure can return to the more-privileged procedure by calling through a gate. Note that this description covers only the rudiments of calling less-privileged procedures. In any given operating system, the actual implementation of such calls may be substantially more complex.

Input/Output

5

CHAPTER 5
INPUT/OUTPUT

The 80386 supports both I/O-mapped and memory-mapped I/O devices. An operating system can restrict I/O operations to itself, or it can allow tasks running at lower privilege levels to read and write selected I/O devices, whether memory- or I/O-mapped. Operating systems can also delegate I/O operations to separate processors, such as DMA (direct memory access) controllers.

5.1 PROGRAMMED I/O

Input/output operations performed by 80386 instructions are called programmed I/O operations. An operating system can address I/O device registers located in either the 80386 dedicated I/O space or in the physical memory space. The 80386 architecture provides special instructions for accessing device registers in the I/O space; ordinary memory reference instructions can be used to read or write memory-mapped devices.

5.1.1 I/O-Mapped I/O

The 80386 IN, OUT, INS, and OUTS instructions refer to device registers mapped into the processor's 64KB I/O space. Each location in the I/O space is called an I/O port; ports can be 8, 16, or 32 bits wide. IN and OUT move a byte, a word, or a dword between the AL/AX/EAX register and an I/O port. INS and OUTS transfer byte, word, or dword strings between an I/O port and memory. A task's ability to issue these I/O instructions is subject to the protection constraints described in Section 5.2.

5.1.2 Memory-Mapped I/O

A memory-mapped device register can be accessed with any memory reference instruction, although MOV, AND, OR, and TEST are the most commonly used. Any memory addressing mode can be used to specify the offset of a memory-mapped device. When using memory-mapped I/O, an operating system designer must observe these cautions:

- Verify that your compiler aligns the structures that you declare to represent device registers to the actual addresses occupied by the registers.

- Beware of the 80386 bit test and bit field instructions (BT, BTS, BTR, and BTC). Regardless of the actual register size, the processor will always initiate a 16- or 32-bit bus cycle to access the operand of these instructions. Before using one of these instructions, be certain that the hardware will complete the bus cycle and that you do not erroneously access adjacent registers, or non-existent physical addresses.

- If your hardware implements a data cache, be sure that it does not cache memory-mapped I/O registers. To see why device registers should not be cached, suppose a task repeatedly polls the status register of a memory-mapped device. The first time the register is polled, the cacheing hardware loads the register value into the cache and the task reads that value. Subsequent polls, however, are likely to obtain the cache value again, even if the real value has changed. (The device has no way to invalidate the cache entry.) One simple way to distinguish between cacheable and noncacheable addresses is to divide the physical address space in half and use address line 31 to distinguish between cacheable and noncacheable addresses. The *80386 Hardware Reference Manual* covers cacheing in detail.

5.2 IOPL AND THE I/O PERMISSION MAP

A memory-mapped device is protected by the attributes encoded in its segment descriptor and, if paging is enabled, the attributes encoded in its PDE and PTE.

5.2.1 Protecting I/O-Mapped Devices

A task's ability to issue an I/O instruction is controlled by its I/O privilege level (IOPL) and its optional I/O guard map. A task can issue an I/O instruction on any I/O port if the task's current privilege level is less than or equal to its IOPL. The processor maintains the running task's IOPL in a like-named field of the EFLAGS register; the value of IOPL can range from 0-3. Because the 80386 loads EFLAGS from the new TSS on every task switch, tasks can have different IOPLs. So long as a task cannot write into its TSS (except by calling operating system procedures), a task cannot change its ability to do I/O. A task running at a privilege level greater than 0 cannot change its IOPL with the unprivileged POPF instruction because this instruction alters IOPL only when CPL=0.

A task's IOPL controls its right to execute these instructions: IN, INS, OUT, OUTS, INT *n*, IRET, PUSHF, POPF, STI, and CLI. Thus, a task whose IOPL allows it to issue I/O instructions can also enable and disable interrupts. Such a task must be highly trusted. An operating system can use a task's I/O permission map to grant a less-trusted task access to selected I/O ports while protecting IF flag from the task.

If a task's CPL is greater than its IOPL, and the task attempts to execute an I/O instruction, the 80386 consults the I/O permission map in the task's TSS. If the permission map allows access to the port named in the instruction, the 80386 executes the instruction; if the permission map denies access to the port, the 80386 raises a general protection exception. To appreciate the utility of an I/O permission map, consider a real-time system that controls a special I/O device for which there is no operating system driver. Setting an application task's IOPL to zero prevents the task from disabling interrupts or accessing arbitrary I/O ports. Yet with an appropriately initialized I/O permission map, the application task, running at any privilege level, can read and write the port(s) that represent the special device and no other ports.

Figure 5-1 shows how the I/O permission map is organized and how the 80386 interprets it. (Note that the I/O permission map is not defined for 80286 TSSs, as the 80286 has no corresponding facility.) An I/O permission map is a bit string up to 64 Kbits in length; each bit represents an address in the 80386 I/O space. A 0-bit permits access to the corresponding I/O address; a 1-bit causes a general protection exception if a task attempts to access

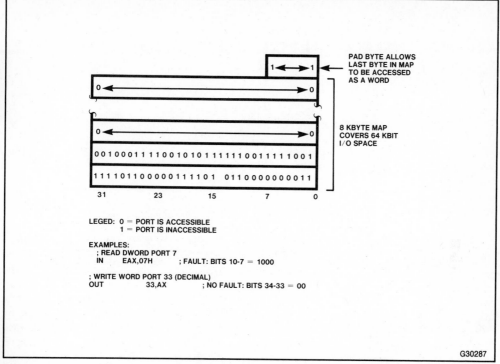

PAD BYTE ALLOWS
LAST BYTE IN MAP
TO BE ACCESSED
AS A WORD

8 KBYTE MAP
COVERS 64 KBIT
I/O SPACE

```
0 0 1 0 0 0 1 1 1 1 0 0 1 0 1 0 1 1 1 1 1 1 0 0 1 1 1 1 1 0 0 1
1 1 1 1 0 1 1 0 0 0 0 0 1 1 1 1 0 1   0 1 1 0 0 0 0 0 0 0 0 0 1 1
31              23              15              7               0
```

LEGED: 0 = PORT IS ACCESSIBLE
        1 = PORT IS INACCESSIBLE

EXAMPLES:
  ; READ DWORD PORT 7
  IN   EAX,07H   ; FAULT: BITS 10-7 = 1000

  ; WRITE WORD PORT 33 (DECIMAL)
  OUT   33,AX   ; NO FAULT: BITS 34-33 = 00

G30287

Figure 5-1. I/O Permission Map Structure and Operation

the corresponding port. As the examples in Figure 5-1 show, a multibyte access is allowed only if all permission bits representing the target word or doubleword port are 0.

Figure 5-2 shows that a task's I/O permission map is located in its TSS above the area used by the operating system, if any. The I/O permission map base field in the TSS must be initialized with the displacement of the map from the base of the TSS. Because the 80386 reads the I/O permission map in units of one word, the last byte of the I/O permission map must be followed by a pad byte containing all 1-bits. Setting the I/O permission map base field in the TSS to FFFFH defines a null permission map. A null map is equivalent to a map containing all 1-bits and requires no pad byte.

The limit field in the TSS descriptor governs the extent of the I/O permission map. The limit field can be used to define a map that is smaller than the 8 Kbytes required to explicitly define the accessibility of all 65,536 I/O addresses. When the I/O permission map is truncated by the limit field, the processor interprets the unspecified bits as 1s, thus prohibiting I/O to any address not defined in the map. Thus, an operating system need only define as much of the map as is needed to specify the addresses to which I/O is permitted. Whatever the I/O permission map's length, it must be terminated with a pad byte of all 1-bits, and the TSS limit field must account for the extra byte. (The 80386 uses word accesses to read the I/O permission map; the pad byte ensures that the last map byte can be read.)

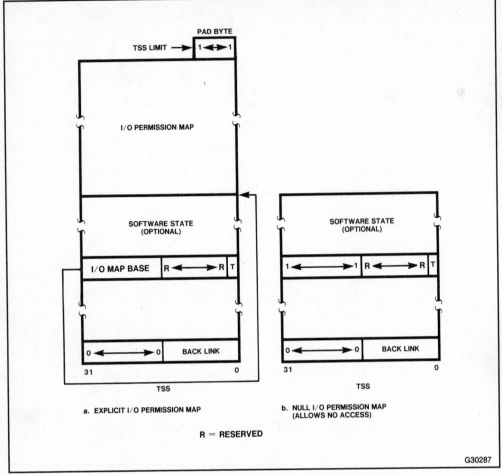

Figure 5-2. I/O Permission Map Location and Extent

5.2.2 Device Driver Privilege

Device drivers that are implemented as procedures should run at privilege level 0. A typical device driver is implemented as an operating system service procedure, an interrupt procedure, and data that describes the device and pending I/O requests. The service procedure runs in he context of the task that requests an I/O operation; the interrupt procedure runs in the context of the task that happens to be executing when the device interrupts. Because the service procedure and the interrupt handler interact with the device and with request data, they share data and call common procedures. If, as is usually desirable, the operating system is to be interruptible at all privilege levels, then the interrupt procedure must be assigned DPL=0. (The 80386 raises a general protection fault if an interrupt attempts to invoke an interrupt procedure whose DPL is greater than the current privilege level.) This means that any procedure the interrupt procedure calls must also have DPL=0. Because the common procedures have DPL=0, the service procedure must also have DPL=0.

Implementing a device driver as a collection of privilege level 0 procedures has the disadvantage of jeopardizing all system code and data whenever a driver is installed or modified. Where performance and protection requirements permit or demand, a device driver can be implemented as two tasks whose procedures run at privilege level 1 or 2. The gain in protection is offset to some degree by a decline in performance, due to the extra time required to invoke an interrupt task, and the need for the driver to make system calls to obtain operating system services (for example, to wake up a task).

5.3 DIRECT I/O

When setting up direct I/O operations, the operating system must accommodate the limitations of the direct I/O processor, typically a DMA controller.

5.3.1 Physical Addressing

Most DMA controllers can generate only physical memory addresses. To support direct memory access, the operating system must supply the DMA controller with the physical address of an I/O buffer. If the operating system allocates buffers statically, it can associate a header record with each buffer and initialize a field in the header with the buffer's physical address. When buffers are allocated dynamically, the operating system can implement a procedure that uses the GDT and LDT (and page directory and page tables, if paging is enabled) to translate a logical address to a physical address.

When paging is enabled, an operating system must be prepared for I/O requests that cross page boundaries. Addresses that are linearly adjacent can be mapped to noncontiguous page frames. Using the page directory and page tables, the operating system can break I/O requests that cross nonadjacent page frames into multiple DMA controller commands.

A DMA controller may also be limited in the amount of physical memory it can address; many controllers, for example, have a range of only 16 megabytes. If the hardware implements more physical memory than the DMA controller can address, the operating system must allocate I/O buffers in the area of physical memory that the DMA controller can address.

5.3.2 Locking Segments and Pages

An operating system must ensure that the physical address and validity of a memory location that is the subject of a direct I/O transfer does not change until the transfer is complete. In practice, this means that a segment or page cannot be moved, deleted, or made not-present while a direct I/O transfer involving the segment or page is pending. Segment descriptors have one available bit that the operating system can designate as meaning "locked for I/O." Page table entries have three available bits that can be used for the same purpose. All operating system code must refrain from altering a locked descriptor or PTE if the alteration would result in an incomplete I/O operation.

Initialization 6

CHAPTER 6
INITIALIZATION

Initialization is the sequence of instructions an operating system must execute before starting the first task. The great bulk of initialization consists of creating operating system data structures and is therefore independent of the 80386. This chapter describes the processor-dependent aspects of initialization, emphasizing three key transitions:

*   Entering protected mode
*   Enabling paging (optional)
*   Switching to the initial task

A good deal of operating system-specific code is likely to be interspersed between these transitions.

6.1 ENTERING PROTECTED MODE

When its RESET line is activated, the 80386 responds by entering real mode. As discussed in Chapter 9, real mode is useful for applications that wish to use the 80386 as a very fast 8086. Most applications, however, are best served by the full resources of the processor; to make these resources available, the operating system initialization code must switch the processor from real mode to protected mode. At about the same time, most operating systems also transfer control to a 32-bit code segment to change the default operand and address sizes to 32 bits. A typical operating system switches from real to protected mode and from a 16-bit to a 32-bit code segment as soon as possible following a RESET.

Table 6-1 show the contents of the 80386's registers immediately following activation of the RESET line. Activation of RESET also forces address lines A31-20 to high for code fetches. These address lines remain high (for code fetches) until an intersegment jump or call is executed; following such an instruction, A31-A20 go low and remain low until the processor is switched to protected mode. Data references following a RESET are directed by default to the first 64 Kbytes of the linear (and physical) address space.

Thus, following a RESET, the 80386 code space is the top 64 Kbytes of the 80386 linear address space, and the data space is the low 64 Kbytes. A simple way to implement a RESET routine is to place both code and data in the top 64 Kbytes and use a CS segment override prefix for data references; this forces data addresses to fall into the top 64 Kbytes of the address space. Such a simple routine must refrain from issuing an intersegment transfer until it has switched the processor from real mode to protected mode.

Given the RESET values of CS, EIP, and address lines A31-A20, the 80386 fetches its first instruction from linear address FFFFFFF0H. Because the RESET address is so close to the code segment limit, the instruction there should be an intrasegment jump to a lower offset in the 64 Kbyte code segment. An attempt to fetch an instruction from past the 64 Kbyte code segment limit produces a general protection exception.

INITIALIZATION

Table 6-1. Registers Following RESET

Register	Value
EFLAGS	Defined bits contain 0; undefined bits contain undefined values
CR0	Defined bits contain 0 except for ET, whose value is described in Chapter 7; undefined bits contain undefined values
CS Base	FFFF0000H
CS Limit	FFFFH
EIP	0000FFF0H
DS-GS Base	00000000H
DS-GS Limit	FFFFH
EAX	Self-test result or undefined[1]
EDX	Component and revision number[1]
All Others	Undefined

[1]For information on self-test and component and revision numbers, consult the *80386 Hardware Reference Manual*.

Figures 6-1 through 6-3 show an assembly language program that illustrates the essentials of switching the 80386 from real to protected mode after a RESET. Figure 6-4 shows how this program would appear if it were burned into ROM. Upon completion of the program, the 80386 is configured as a "flat" unprotected machine with a 32-bit address space.

The program shown in Figures 6-1 through 6-3 has limitations that an actual initialization routine can avoid:

- The program leaves a large unused space between its first and last instructions; a different program could locate the instructions and data closer to the RESET address.

- The program defines descriptors by encoding their actual bit values. While practical in a simple program like this, operating systems that define many static descriptors may be able to use the Intel System Builder utility to advantage. The Builder can create the IDT, the GDT, LDTs, and TSSs from symbolic specifications. A simple bootstrap loader can transfer these images from disk to RAM, or they can be burned into ROM and then copied to RAM.

The comments in Figures 6-1 through 6-3 explain the operation of the program, but a few points should be noted:

- The program is written as two segments called ResetSeg and BigSeg. ResetSeg contains 8086-compatible code while BigSeg contains 32-bit 80386 code. Where an 80386 instruction must be executed in ResetSeg (for example, MOV CR0,EAX), the assembler automatically provides the required override prefix.

```
; THIS CODE HAS NOT BEEN TESTED
; Initialize 80386 to flat 32-bit machine

ResetSeg segment
; locate this segment (e.g., with Binder) to 0FFFF0000H

; tell assembler what's in CS
assume CS:ResetSeg

; place first instruction at RESET address 0FFFFFFF0H
          org     0FFF0H
RESET:    JMP     Begin

; set location counter to start of ROM
          org     8000H

STARTROMTABS      label    word    ; tag start of ROM tables
; define GDT containing required null descriptor plus one
; descriptor for code and one descriptor for data

ROMGDT   label    word
NullDes  dw       0,0,0,0
CodeDes  dw       0FFFFH              ; limit at max (bits 15:0)
         db       0,0,0               ; base at 0 (bits 23:0)
         db       10011011B           ; present/DPL 0/code/
                                      ; nonconform/readable/X
         db       11001111B           ; 4K grain/default 32/
                                      ; 0/X/limit (bits 19:16)
         db       0                   ; base at 0 (bits 31:24)
DataDes  dw       0FFFFH              ; limit at max (bits 15:0)
         db       0,0,0               ; base at 0 (bits 23:0)
         db       10010011B           ; present/DPL 0/data/
                                      ; expand-up/writeable/X
         db       10001111B           ; 4K grain/00/X/
                                      ; limit (bits 19:16)
         db       0                   ; base at 0 (bits 31:24)
```

Figure 6-1. Entering Protected Mode (Part 1)

• Immediately after switching to protected mode, the program issues a JMP instruction to flush the instructions in the 80386 prefetch queue. The instructions in the queue were fetched and decoded while the processor was in real mode; executing them after it has been switched to protected mode can be erroneous. For example, the 80386 loads a segment register differently in real mode than in protected mode.

The 80386 can be switched from protected to real mode; this subject is discussed in Chapter 9.

```
; define IDT
ROMIDT   label word
; up to 256 interrupt/trap gates go here
ENDROMTABS label      word    ; tag end of rom tables

; define values for IDT and GDT registers
IDTPtr   dw      7FFH        ; limit is max for 256 interrupts
         dw      offset IDT  ; base (bits 15:0) is IDT base
         dw      0FFFFH      ; base (bits 31:16) is IDT base

GDTPtr   dw      17H         ; limit is 3: null, code, and data
         dw      offset GDT  ; base (bits 15:0) is GDT base
         dw      0FFFFH      ; base (bits 31:16) is GDT base

Begin    ; still in real mode, use CS override for data refs
         ; disable interrupts in case we aren't starting from RESET
         CLI
         ; move GDT and IDT to RAM with string move
         MOV     SI,offset CS:STARTROMTABS     ; set source
         MOV     DI,offset CS:TABLES           ; set destination
         MOV     CX,ENDROMTABS-STARTROMTABS    ; set byte count
         CLD                  ; auto-increment
         DTOV    DS,CS
         MOV     ES,CS        ; initialize ES for string move
         REP     MOVSB        ; move tables
         LIDT    CS:IDTPtr    ; load IDTR
         LGDT    CS:GDTPtr    ; load GDTR
         MOV     EAX,CR0      ; get current CR0
         MOV     EAX,1B       ; set PE bit
         MOV     CR0,EAX      ; begin protected mode
; flush prefetch queue
         JMP     Continue
```

Figure 6-2. Entering Protected Mode (Part 2)

6.2 ENABLING PAGING

Before enabling paging, the 80386 must be running in protected mode. An operating system must also ensure that the data structures and routines associated with paging are in place:

- A page directory must contain present PDEs for at least the page table(s) that cover the pages containing the page fault handler.

- The page fault handler must be present in physical memory; its presence must be reflected in the page table(s) that map its addresses.

- Entry 14 of the IDT must contain a descriptor (normally a trap gate) that points to the page fault handler.

- The code and data that enable paging must be in present pages and their linear addresses must be equal to their physical addresses; that is, they must identify mapped.

```
Continue:
; now in protected mode
; set data segment registers to DataDes
        MOV      BX,10H              ; load DataDes selector
        MOV      SS,BX
        MOV      DS,BX
        MOV      ES,BX

; load CS with CodeDes
        JMP      far ptr Start32 ; intersegment jump
; set location counter to start of RAM in this segment
        ORG      0H

; allocate RAM for GDT and IDT
TABLES  label    word
GDT     db       dup(3*8)            ; space for 3 descriptors
IDT     db       dub(256*8)          ; space for 256 descriptors

ResetSeg ends                        ; end of segment
BigSeg   segment use32
; this segment should be located at linear address 0

assume CS:BigSeg,DS:BigSeg,ES:BigSeg,SS:BigSeg

Start32:
; code here can load ESP with top of stack pointer,
; enable interrupts, and proceed with initialization.

BigSeg   ends
```

Figure 6-3. Entering Protected Mode (Part 3)

Disk copies of any pages marked not-present must be up-to-date before enabling paging. With data and code in place, the operating system issues a MOV CR3 instruction to load the *physical* address of the page directory into the page directory base register. To enable paging, the operating system can set the PG bit (bit 31 of CR0) without disturbing other bits in CR0 as follows:

```
MOV    EAX,CR0
OR     EAX,80000000H
MOV    CR0,EAX
JMP    anywhere
```

Note the JMP instruction following the MOV instruction that enables paging. (There are no restrictions on the address of the jump target.) This instruction flushes the prefetch queue; the prefetch queue may contain instructions whose operand addresses were computed before paging was enabled. Executing these instructions after paging has been enabled is erroneous unless their operands have identical linear and physical addresses. Flushing the prefetch queue immediately after enabling paging eliminates any potential problem.

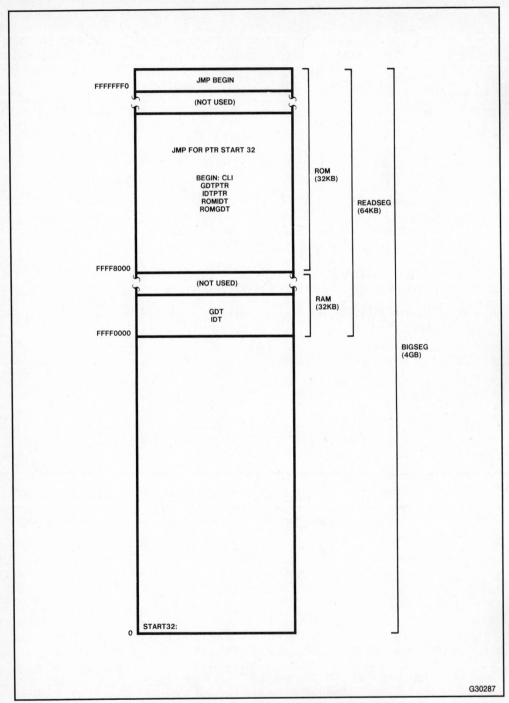

FFFFFFF0 — JMP BEGIN

(NOT USED)

JMP FOR PTR START 32

BEGIN: CLI
GDTPTR
IDTPTR
ROMIDT
ROMGDT

FFFF8000

(NOT USED)

GDT
IDT

FFFF0000

START32:

0

ROM
(32KB)

RAM
(32KB)

READSEG
(64KB)

BIGSEG
(4GB)

G30287

Figure 6-4. Entering Protected Mode Program Layout

6.3 SWITCHING TO THE INITIAL TASK

Before switching to the first task, the operating system must create a valid TSS and TSS descriptor for the first task, and a dummy TSS and valid TSS descriptor for the running pseudotask. The 80386 writes its machine state into the dummy TSS when the operating system switches to the first task. With the TSSs in place, the operating system can issue the LTR instruction to load the task register with a selector for the dummy TSS descriptor. To effect the actual task switch, the operating system can issue the usual JMP TSS instruction.

Numerics 7

CHAPTER 7
NUMERICS

An 80386 numerics instruction (defined in the next paragraph) can be executed directly by an 80387 or 80287 Numerics Coprocessor, or interpreted by a software emulator that mimics one of these coprocessors. Functionally, all three options are nearly identical; they differ primarily in speed. The operating system support required for any of them is fairly simple and is limited to initialization, task switching, and exception handling functions.

In this chapter, the term "numerics instruction" refers to those valid instructions that the 80386 cannot execute itself. The most common numerics instructions operate on real ("floating point") data types, but there are also packed decimal and integer instructions. In ASM386, numerics instruction mnemonics begin with the letter F, such as FADD, FMUL, and FSQRT. Numerics machine instructions begin with the pattern 11011B, which is called the ESC (escape) opcode.

7.1 SUPPORTING A COPROCESSOR

A numerics coprocessor is essentially a parallel execution unit that interprets numerics instructions. A coprocessor performs no bus transactions, but instead relies on the 80386 to compute addresses, to fetch instructions, and to load and store memory-based operands. Because it is little more than an extended execution unit, a numerics coprocessor places little additional burden on an operating system. The additional support consists mainly of telling the 80386 that a numerics coprocessor is present, and responding to two exceptions that the 80386 raises in behalf of the coprocessor.

7.1.1 Initialization

During its initialization phase, an operating system must determine which numerics coprocessor is present, inform the 80386 of this, and initialize the coprocessor before executing any numerics instructions.

The operating system's initialization code can tell if an 80387 is present by testing the ET (extension type) bit in CR0; as part of its RESET sequence, the 80386 sets this bit if an 80387 is present. Testing for an 80287 can be almost as easy. The code fragment shown in Figure 7-1 will probe for a numerics chip in a pc, and will work with 8086/8087, 80286/80287, 80386/80287, or 80386/80387.

Having determined which numerics coprocessor is present, the operating system's initialization code must set up the 80386. This consists of setting the values of the EM (emulate coprocessor) and MP (monitor coprocessor) bits in CR0. Table 7-1 shows how the 80386 interprets these bits. The EM bit directs the 80386 to pass numerics instructions to either a coprocessor (EM=0) or to an emulator (EM=1). The MP bit directs the 80386 to ignore (MP=0) or to test (MP=1) the TS (task switched) bit before executing an 80386 WAIT instruction. The MP bit is provided for compatibility with 8086-based systems that used the WAIT instruction to synchronize with a device (other than a numerics coprocessor) connected

```
DOS 3.20 (033-N) 8086/87/88/186 MACRO ASSEMBLER V2.0 ASSEMBLY OF MODULE TEST-NPX
OBJECT MODULE PLACED IN FINDNPX.OBJ
ASSEMBLER INVOKED BY: D:\ASM86.EXE FINDNPX.A86

LOC  OBJ              LINE    SOURCE

                      1  +1   $title('Test for presence of an Numerics Chip')
                      2
                      3          name    Test-NPX
                      4          extrn   dqopen:near,dqcreate:near,dqwrite:near,dqexit:near
                      5
000D                  6   CR    EQU     0DH
000A                  7   LF    EQU     0AH
                      8
----                  9   stack segment stack 'stack'
0000 (100            10          dw      100 dup (?)
     ????
     )
00C8 ????            11   sst   dw      ?                    ; Top of stack label
----                 12   stack ends
                     13
----                 14   data  segment public 'data'
0000 0000            15   status dw     0
0000 0000            16   co    dw      0
0000 0000            17   temp  dw      0
0007 3A434F3A        18   co-name db    4,':CO:'
000B 21              19   n-npx db      33,'No 8087, 80287, or 80387 found.',CR,LF
000C 4E6F2038303837
     2C20383032383037
     2C206F7220383030
     3338372066666F75
     6E642E
002B 0D
002C 0A
002D 11              20   f_387 db      17,'Found an 80387.',CR,LF
```

Figure 7-1. Probing for an 80287

```
DOS 3.20 (033-N) 8086/87/88/186 MACRO ASSEMBLER V2.0 ASSEMBLY OF MODULE TEST_NPX
OBJECT MODULE PLACED IN FINDNPX.OBJ
ASSEMBLER INVOKED BY: D:\ASM86.EXE FINDNPX.A86

LOC   OBJ               LINE   SOURCE

002E  466F756E642061           21    f_npx   db    25,'Found an 8087 or 80287.',CR,LF
      6E203830333837
      2E
003D  0D
003E  0A
003F  19
0040  466F756E642061
      6E20383038383720
      6F72203830323238
      372E
0057  0D
0058  0A
----                     22    data   ends
                         23 +1 $eject
                         24    dgroup group data,stack
                         25    cgroup group code
                         26
----                     27    code   segment public 'code'
                         28           assume cs:cgroup,ds:dgroup
                         29
                         30    start:
0000  B8----         R   31           mov    ax,dgroup
0003  8ED8               32           mov    ds,ax
0005  8ED0               33           mov    ss,ax
0007  BCC800         R   34           mov    sp,offset dgroup:st
000A  B80600         R   35           mov    ax,offset dgroup:co-name
000D  50                 36           push   ax
000E  B80000         R   37           mov    ax,offset dgroup:status
0011  50                 38           push   ax
0012  E80000         E   39           call   dqcreate   ; Setup file connection
0015  A30200         R   40           mov    co,ax      ; Save file token
0018  50                 41           push   ax
0019  B80200             42           mov    ax,2       ; Signal write open
```

Figure 7-1. Probing for an 80287 (Cont'd.)

```
DOS 3.20 (033-N) 8086/87/88/186 MACRO ASSEMBLER V2.0 ASSEMBLY OF MODULE TEST-NPX
OBJECT MODULE PLACED IN FINDNPX.OBJ
ASSEMBLER INVOKED BY: D:\ASM86.EXE FINDNPX.A86


LOC   OBJ        LINE   SOURCE

001C  50           43       push    ax
001D  33C0         44       xor     ax,ax       ; No buffers needed
001F  50           45       push    ax
0020  B800000  R   46       mov     ax,offset dgroup:status
0023  50           47       push    ax
0024  E80000   E   48       call    dqopen      ; Open file for writing
0027  FF360200 R   49       push    co          ; Setup for call
002B  BB0B00   R   50       mov     bx,offset dgroup:n-npx
002E  EB18         51       jmp     short test-npx ; Enter test code on next page
                   52       ;
                   53       ; Print message at [BX] then exit
                   54       ;
0030                55   found_87_287:
0030  BB3F00   R   56       mov     bx,offset dgroup:f-npx
                   57   no-npx:
0033               58   found_387:
0033  43           59       inc     bx          ; Point at character string
0034  53           60       push    bx
0035  8A47FF       61       mov     al,[bx-1]   ; Get count
0038  98           62       cbw
0039  50           63       push    ax
003A  B80000   R   64       mov     ax,offset dgroup:status
003D  50           65       push    ax
003E  E80000   E   66       call    dqwrite     ; Print message
0041  33c0         67       xor     ax,ax
0043  50           68       push    ax
0044  E80000   E   69       call    dqexit      ; End the program, go back to DOS
0047  CC           70       int     3           ; Just in case
                   71  +1 $eject
                   72       ;
                   73       ; Look for an 8087, 80287, or 80387 NPX.
                   74       ; Note that we cannot execute WAIT on 8086/88 if no 8087 is present.
                   75       ;
                   76   test-npx:

0048
```

Figure 7-1. Probing for an 80287 (Cont'd.)

```
DOS 3.20 (033-N) 8086/87/88/186 MACRO ASSEMBLER V2.0 ASSEMBLY OF MODULE TEST_NPX
OBJECT MODULE PLACED IN FINDNPX.OBJ
ASSEMBLER INVOKED BY:  D:\ASM86.EXE FINDNPX.A86

LOC  OBJ        LINE  SOURCE

0048 90DBE3       77    fninit              ; Must use non-wait form
004B BE0400       78 R  mov    si,offset dgroup:temp
004E C7045A5A     79    mov    word ptr [si],5A5AH ; Initialize temp to non-zero value
0052 90DD3C       80    fnstsw [si]         ; Must use non-wait form of fstsw
                  81                        ; It is not necessary to use a WAIT instruction
                  82                        ; after fnstsw or fnstcw. Do not use one here.
0055 803C00       83    cmp    byte ptr [si],0 ; See if correct status with zeroes was
                                                read
0058 75D9         84    jne    no-npx       ; Jump if not a valid status word, meaning no
                                                NPX
                  85
                  86    Now see if ones can be correctly written from the control word.
                  87
005A 90D93C       88    fnstcw [si]         ; Look at the control word do not use WAIT form
                  89                        ; Do not use a WAIT instruction here!
005D 8B04         90    mov    ax,[si]      ; See if ones can be written by NPX
005F 253F10       91    and    ax,103fh     ; See if selected parts of control word look OK
0062 3D3F00       92    cmp    ax,3fh       ; Check that ones and zeroes were correctly read
0065 75CC         93    jne    no-npx       ; Jump if no npx is installed
                  94
                  95    Some numerics chip is installed. NPX instructions and WAIT are now
                  96    safe. See if the NPX is an 8087/287 or 80387.
                  97    This code is necessary if a denormal exception handler is
                  98    used or the new 80387 instructions will be used.
                  99
0067 9BD9E8      100    fld1                ; Must use default control word from FNINIT
006A 9BD9EE      101    fldz                ; Form infinity
006D 9BDEF9      102    fdiv                ; 8087/287 says +inf = -inf
0070 9BD9C0      103    fld    st           ; Form negative infinity
0073 9BD9E0      104    fchs                ; 80387 says +inf <> -inf
```

Figure 7-1. Probing for an 80287 (Cont'd.)

```
DOS 3.20 (033-N) 8086/87/88/186 MACRO ASSEMBLER V2.0 ASSEMBLY OF MODULE TEST_NPX
OBJECT MODULE PLACED IN FINDNPX.OBJ
ASSEMBLER INVOKED BY: D:\ASM86.EXE FINDNPX.A86


LOC  OBJ          LINE   SOURCE

0076 9BDED9       105         fcompp            ; See if they are the same and remove them
0079 9BDD3C       106         fstsw   [si]      ; Look at status from FCOMPP
007C 8B04         107         mov     ax,[si]
007E 9E           108         sahf              ; See if the infinities matched
007F 74AF         109         je      found_87_287 Jump if 8087/287 is present
                  110    ;
                  111    ;      An 80387 is present. If denormal exceptions are used for an
                  112    ;      8087/287, they must be masked. The 80387 will automatically
                  113    ;      normalize denormal operands faster than an exception handler can.
                  114    ;
0081 BB2D00     R 115         mov     bx,offset dgroup:f_387
0084 EBAD         116         jmp     found_387
                  117    code   ends
                  118         end     start,ds:dgroup,ss:dgroup:sst
                  119

ASSEMBLY COMPLETE, NO ERRORS FOUND
```

Figure 7-1. Probing for an 80287 (Cont'd.)

NUMERICS

Table 7-1. EM and MP Bit Interpretation

EM	MP	Interpretation
0	0	Numerics instructions are passed to coprocessor; WAIT ignores TS
0	1	Numerics instructions are passed to coprocessor; WAIT tests TS
1	0	Numerics instructions trap to emulator; WAIT ignores TS
1	1	Numerics instructions trap to emulator; WAIT tests TS

to the BUSY# line. If numerics instructions can be encountered in a system, EM and MP must be set to 0 and 1, respectively, for coprocessor interpretation of the instructions, or to 1 and 1 for emulator interpretation.

EM and MP can be altered with the privileged MOV CR0 instruction. To avoid altering other bits in the register (for example, the ET bit), a sequence like the following can be used.

```
MOV    EAX,CR0
AND    EAX,BitClearMask
OR     EAX,BitSetMask
MOV    CR0,EAX
```

The WAIT instruction always waits for the BUSY# pin to go inactive; however, if no coprocessor is present, a pullup resistor in the 80386 causes WAIT to continue immediately as if BUSY# were inactive. The WAIT instruction is used to delay execution of the next 80386 instruction while a coprocessor stores data in memory. WAIT is an interruptible instruction; upon return from an interrupt handler the processor resumes execution of the WAIT instruction.

The FNINIT instruction initializes the coprocessor; it must be the first numerics instruction every task executes (the operating system can issue the instruction for an application task). (FRSTOR can also be used to initialize the coprocessor if the restored coprocessor state record contains the same values that FNINIT produces; FRSTOR, however, takes substantially longer to execute than FNINIT.) The FSETPM instruction, required when the 80287 is used with an 80286, is not required when either coprocessor is used with an 80386; the 80386 ignores FSETPM. (The 80386 maintains and formats the addresses of the current numerics instruction and operand, so neither coprocessor need be concerned with the 80386's mode.)

For every task that issues a numerics instruction, the operating system must provide space to save the coprocessor's state on task switches. Because, in general, it is not practical to know which tasks execute numerics instructions and which do not, it is best to provide coprocessor save areas for all tasks if a numerics coprocessor or emulator is present. A convenient place for this save area is the software state area of the task's TSS; for best performance the save area should be doubleword-aligned. The save area should be 94 bytes, the size of the area used by the FSAVE and FRSTOR instructions.

7.1.2 Exceptions

With respect to numerics instructions, the 80386 raises an exception to notify system software of the following:

- A task switch has occurred since execution of the previous numerics instruction; therefore, the context of the coprocessor may have to be switched before executing the current numerics instruction.
- The previous numerics instruction incurred an error that requires software intervention.
- A numerics instruction must be emulated.

Chapter 3 describes the 80386's exception facilities in general; the following sections discuss the two exceptions that relate specifically to numerics coprocessors.

7.1.2.1 COPROCESSOR CONTEXT SWITCHING

A numerics coprocessor adds considerable machine state to a task, the bulk of it consisting of either 80-bit registers. The operating system dispatcher can switch the coprocessor context on every task switch. In most applications, however, this expensive operation is often wasted because ordinarily only a minority of tasks issue numerics instructions. The coprocessor context must actually be switched only when the task state loaded in the coprocessor does not represent the task about to execute a numerics instruction. This may be simpler to understand by defining the notion of "numerics tasks," that is, the subset of tasks that actually issue numerics instructions. The context of the coprocessor must be changed only when the current numerics task is not the same as the previous numerics task. By changing the context of the coprocessor only when a different numerics task issues a numerics instruction, many task switches can be made without incurring the expense of saving and reloading the context of the coprocessor.

To help implement this strategy, the 80386 sets the TS bit in CR0 whenever it performs a task switch. It also tests TS before executing any numerics instruction; when MP is set, the 80386 further tests TS before executing a WAIT instruction. If, when tested, TS is set, the processor raises exception number 7 (device not available). This exception means that at least one task switch has occurred since the execution of the previous numerics or WAIT instruction. The exception handler should therefore determine if the task whose context is represented in the coprocessor (that is, the previous task to issue a numerics instruction) is not the task whose attempt to execute a numerics instruction just incurred the exception. The tasks may actually be the same; suppose, for example, that numerics Task A issues a numerics instruction and is shortly thereafter preempted by Task B. Task B, which is non-numeric, runs for awhile and then gives up the processor, allowing Task A to run again. When Task A next issues a numerics instruction, the 80386 raises exception 7 because there have been two task switches (A to B and B to A) since the previous numerics instruction was executed. Nevertheless, the context of the coprocessor is still Task B's context, and there is no need to change it before Task B executes another instruction. In this case, the exception handler need only reset the TS bit and IRET. If, on the other hand, the running task is not the same as the task whose context is loaded in the coprocessor, the handler must save the coprocessor context in the old task's coprocessor save area and reload it from the new task's

Exception 16 is a trap, not a fault. On entry to the handler, the EIP value on the stack does not point to the offending instruction. It points to the numerics instruction or WAIT *following* the offending instruction (that is, to the instruction the processor was starting to execute when it noticed that ERROR# was active). To examine the offending instruction (and, if applicable, its memory operand), the handler can issue the FSTENV instruction.

A coprocessor error handler can terminate the offending task, can supply an alternate result, or can change a source operand and reexecute the instruction. To reexecute an instruction, the handler can copy the offending instruction to a data segment for which the handler has an alias that redefines the data segment as a code segment. By following the copied instruction with a RET instruction, the handler can CALL the instruction and then regain control.

7.1.2.3 SIMULTANEOUS EXCEPTIONS

As it begins to execute a numerics instruction, the 80386 may find that TS is set and ERROR# is active simultaneously. In this case, the processor raises exception 7 first. What happens next depends on whether the exception 7 handler switched the context of the coprocessor. If it did not, as soon as the exception 7 handler returns, the 80386 raises exception 16. If the exception 7 handler switched the coprocessor context, the fact that an error was pending in the old task is saved in its TSS by the FSAVE instruction. When the context of the old task is next reloaded with FRSTOR, the coprocessor immediately activates ERROR#. As a result, the next time the old task issues a numerics instruction, the 80386 raises exception 16. In sum, task switching takes priority over numerics error handling, but the exception 16 handler is always properly invoked in the context of the task that incurred the error.

7.1.3 Coprocessor Differences

When attached to an 80386, the 80287 and 80387 are essentially identical from an application programming point of view. Both coprocessors automatically support real, protected, and virtual 86 mode operation. Aside from speed, the most visible difference between the processors is the few additional instructions provided by the 80387. Should the 80386 encounter an instruction that the 80287 cannot execute (because it is a member of the expanded 80387 instruction set), the processor nevertheless passes the instruction on to the coprocessor. The 80287's interpretation of such an instruction is not defined.

Other differences between the 80287 and 80387 are masked by the 80386. For example, when attached to an 80286, the 80287 can overrun a segment when fetching or storing a multiword operand; the result is exception 9. However, this never occurs when the coprocessor is used with the 80386; instead the 80386 raises a general protection fault before passing the instruction to the coprocessor.

7.2 SUPPORTING AN EMULATOR

In an application needs the numerics coprocessor instruction set and can accept substantially reduced performance, it can employ software that emulates one of the coprocessors. The Intel emulators mimic their respective coprocessors with great fidelity; the operating system need deal with the emulator only in its initialization code and in the fault handler for exception 7. These subjects are discussed in the following sections.

7.2.1 Initialization

If, at initialization time, the operating system discovers that neither an 80287 nor an 80387 is present, the operating system should direct the 80386 to raise a processor extension not available fault (number 7) if the processor decodes a numerics instruction.

To direct the 80386 to raise exception 7 when it decodes a numerics instruction, the operating system initialization code must set the EM bit in CR0. As discussed in the next section, the handler for exception 7 can either call an emulator or can terminate the task that issued the numerics instruction. If the operating system provides a coprocessor emulator, it can initialize the emulator just as it would initialize a coprocessor, with an FNINIT instruction; the emulator will emulate the instruction. When an emulator is present, the operating system must supply each task with a save area in which the emulator's context can be saved on task switches.

7.2.2 Exceptions

A numerics coprocessor emulator should be packaged as a procedure (or collection of procedures) called by the exception 7 handler when no coprocessor is present. The 80386 raises exception 7 (device not available) when EM is set and the processor encounters a numerics instruction. The processor raises the same exception to notify the operating system that the emulator context may need to be switched. The exception 7 handler can determine whether to call the emulator or to call the coprocessor context switcher by inspecting the EM bit in the EFLAGS image on the stack (EM=0 means call context switcher). If the operating system does not provide an emulator, the exception 7 fault handler should terminate the task.

For anyone contemplating writing a numerics coprocessor emulator, at entry to the exception 7 handler, EIP on the stack points to the instruction, including any prefixes, that must be emulated. As it interprets the instruction, the emulator must increment EIP on the stack so that when the handler returns with an IRET instruction, EIP points to the instruction following the emulated instruction. To emulate an instruction, the emulator must have a descriptor for the associated code segment that grants the emulator read and execute permission; the emulator must be able to read the instruction to emulate it. Pages are always readable, so they require no special attention.

Exception 16 can be handled identically whether numerics instructions are interpreted by an emulator or a coprocessor.

80286 Compatibility

CHAPTER 8
80286 COMPATIBILITY

This chapter describes two ways to execute 80286 binary programs (load modules) on a comparable 80386-based system. The 80386 is almost exactly compatible with the 80286 and can therefore run most 80286 operating systems and applications with little or no change. However, running an 80286 operating system binary does not take advantage of advanced 80386 facilities, because the processor is being used essentially as 80286. The alternative, also described in this chapter, is to develop an 80386 operating system that can support both existing 80286 programs and new 80386 programs. In this way, the operating system and new applications can exploit the features of the 80386 while the investment represented by existing 80286 programs is preserved.

8.1 RUNNING AN 80286 OPERATING SYSTEM

The 80286 data types, registers, instructions, gates, descriptors, and selectors are a proper subset of the corresponding 80386 facilities. An 80286 operating system binary that observes the compatibility rules set forth in the *80286 Programmer's Reference Manual*, can run without modification on the 80386. The most important requirement for 80286-80386 compatibility is the 0 in the top word of 80286 descriptors; non-0 values in this word denote 80386 descriptors. Some other differences between the two processors are listed below; for a definitive list, consult the *80386 Programmer's Reference Manual*. Most of the differences between the processors affect at most isolated portions of operating system code.

• The 80386 stores different values in some fields that were reserved or undefined by the 80286. For example, the 80286 SIDT instruction stores the 40-bit value of the IDTR in a 48-bit field, setting the undefined upper 8 bits to FFH. When it executes the same instruction, the 80386 stores 00H in the upper 8 bits. 80286 programs that relied on values of such reserved or undefined fields may behave differently on the 80386.

• The 80286 and 80386 interpret the LOCK prefix differently. On the 80386, LOCK is independent of IOPL and can only be executed at privilege level 0, and only for a subset of instructions. If LOCK is executed incorrectly on the 80386, the result is an invalid opcode fault. See the *80386 Programmer's Reference Manual* for details.

• The 80386 automatically senses the presence of an 80387; 80286 initialization code that tested for the presence of an 80287 must be changed if an 80387 can be present.

The 80386 has no "80286 mode" analogous to the real mode that emulates an 8086. In protected mode, the processor interprets an instruction according to the content of the descriptors that are in effect at the time the instruction is executed. For example, suppose a JMP instruction's target is 100,000 bytes from the beginning of its code segment. The instruction faults if the code segment was produced by an 80286 translator because the code segment's limit is, at most, 64 Kbytes. The same instruction does not fault if the descriptor specifies a larger limit (as can be the case if the segment is created by an 80386 translator). Thus, code segments are self-identifying: they establish either an 80286 or an 80386 "execution environment" for each instruction. Note, however, that the 80386 does not trap an attempt by a 80286 code segment to execute an 80386 instruction that is undefined for the 80286.

8.2 RUNNING 80286 AND 80386 PROGRAMS CONCURRENTLY

Because the 80386 instructions, data types, and so on are a superset of the 80286's, you can write an 80386 operating system that supports application programs written for the 80386 as well as programs written for a predecessor 80286 operating system.

8.2.1 Basic Operating System Support

Any new operating system that is to support existing applications must maintain a system call interface that is functionally equivalent to the interface provided by the predecessor operating system. At the same time, the new operating system can extend the interface (that is, add system calls or parameters) for the benefit of the new 80386 applications.

Beyond supporting the old application interface, an operating system that supports execution of both 80286 and 80386 programs must recognize that, in general, both old (80286 code) and new (80386 code) tasks can be interrupted or encounter an exception at any time. Consequently, the operating system must

- Use 80386 TSSs for all tasks, whether they are executing 80286 or 80386 programs
- Use only 80386 gates in the IDT
- Use only 80386 code segments for interrupt and exception procedures

In other words, both tasks and interrupt and exception procedures must run in a uniform 80386 "execution environment" to ensure that the processor saves and restores a task's full state whenever the task is interrupted or incurs an exception. (In fact, if an interrupted task is running an 80286 program, more than its full state is saved and restored, but the extra information does not affect the task's behavior.) The uniform environment also ensures that the processor properly invokes and returns from interrupt and exception procedures. For example, an interrupt or exception procedure that returns through an 80386 gate returns control correctly to an 80386 task and incorrectly to an 80286 task (it pops too much information from the stack).

A TSS that represents a task executing an 80286 program should be initialized as follows:

- Set the high word of all doubleword register fields to 0H
- Set CR3 as it is set for tasks executing 80386 programs
- Set the FS and GS fields to 0H (null selector)

The operating system can mark the TSSs of 80386 tasks that are executing 80286 code so that interrupt, exception, and system call handlers can identify the caller, if necessary. (The software state area of the TSS can be used for this purpose.) Note also that the I/O permission map (described in Chapter 5) available in an 80386 TSS can be used to grant 80286 tasks access to selected I/O ports.

8.2.2 Handling Mixed System Calls

80286 code can call an 80386 operating system that provides an interface that is functionally compatible with the interface provided by the 80286 operating system. However, 16-bit parameters and 32-bit results are likely to have to be converted by procedures called system call adapters. In this section, terms such as "80286 code" and "80286 procedure" mean code that is produced by an 80286 translator and that resides in a code segment whose D bit (default operand and address size is 16).

8.2.2.1 SYSTEM CALL ADAPTERS

Figure 8-1 shows how a system call adapter can be positioned so it intercepts system calls from 80286 code without slowing calls from 80386 code. The adapter should be placed behind an 80386 call gate that replaces the 80286 gate formerly used to enter the operating system. (As explained in the next section, 80286 code should call an 80386 operating system through an 80386 gate.) The adapter should have the same privilege level as the operating system. An 80286 task then calls through a gate as usual, but the adapter intercepts the call, converts parameters, and calls the 80386 operating system. The operating system returns to the adapter, which converts results and returns through the gate to the 80286 application code. To avoid interception by the adapter, a task executing 80386 code can call through a different gate.

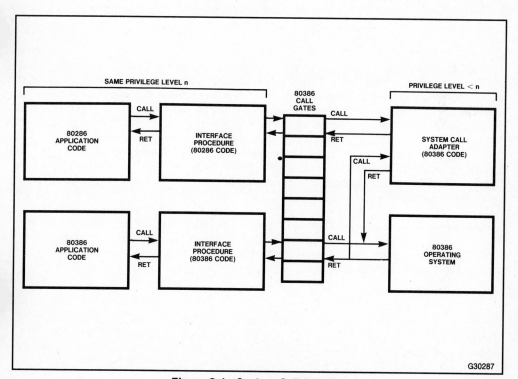

Figure 8-1. System Call Adapter

The adapter must reside in an 80386 code segment whose D bit is 1. The operation of the CALL and RET instructions, when directed to a call gate, are determined by the gate itself. Thus, when an 80286 segment issues a CALL whose operand selects an 80386 call gate, the processor executes the CALL just as if an 80386 segment had issued it. The RET instruction works analogously. Note that because the 80286 code calls through an 80386 gate, the adapter entry point can be at an offset higher than 64 Kbytes (the maximum offset "reachable" with an 80386 gate).

8.2.2.2 PARAMETER PASSING

80286 parameters can be copied automatically through an 80386 call gate, provided that the parameters consist of an even number of words. Whereas an 80286 call gate passes n words (where n is the word count field in the gate), an 80386 call gate passes dwords. If the 80386 gate is defined to pass $n/2$ dwords, the parameters will be copied correctly.

If an 80286 procedure passes an odd number of words, the 80386 gate can be defined to pass zero dwords, and the system call adapter behind the gate can copy the parameters.

8.2.2.3 PARAMETER CONVERSION

80286 offsets and pointers are smaller than the corresponding 80386 types, and the 80386 supports 32-bit integers while the 80286 does not. Thus, 16-bit parameters passed directly from an 80286 program to an 80386 operating system would be misinterpreted by an operating system that expected 32-bit quantities. The system call adapter must convert these parameters to the form expected by the 80386 operating system.

An 8- or 16-bit unsigned value can be converted to 32 bits by adding 0 bits at the high end, using, for example, the MOVZX (move with zero extension) instruction. A 16-bit integer can be converted to 32 bits by propagating its sign bit through the upper bits, using, for example, the MOVSX (move with sign extension) instruction. Floating point numbers need not be converted because they are identical on both processors.

Converting 32-bit results to 16-bit results is similarly straightforward, providing the operating system does not return significant digits in bits 16-31. If a result can legitimately be 32 bits if the caller is a task running 80386 code, the operating system can provide separate system calls for 80286 and 80386 callers.

The adapter or the operating system itself should also ensure that the operating system does not violate protection that would have been enforced had the application been run on an 80286. For example, the operating system should refuse a request from an 80286 program to extend a segment past 64 Kbytes.

8086 Compatibility 9

CHAPTER 9
8086 COMPATIBILITY

The 80386 can execute 8086 binary programs in either of two modes, real mode or virtual 8086 (V86) mode. Real mode is an alternative to protected mode, the mode that has been described in previous chapters. In real mode, the processor behaves much like a fast 8086; it provides no tasking or protection facilities. V86 mode is a submode of protected mode that an operating system can apply to individual 80386 tasks. Virtual 8086 mode provides a protected task environment in which an 8086 program can execute without interfering with the operating system or with other tasks. Thus, whereas real mode governs the execution of all software, virtual 8086 mode applies only when the processor is executing V86 tasks.

Note that some 8086 programs time the duration of a sequence of instructions. Such programs must be modified to execute correctly in real mode or in virtual 8086 mode because the 80386 executes instructions faster than the 8086.

9.1 COMMON ELEMENTS OF REAL AND VIRTUAL 8086 MODES

Real mode and virtual 8086 mode differ most importantly in privilege level and in interrupt and exception handling. In basic instruction execution and addressing, real and V86 modes are quite similar, as described in this section.

9.1.1 Instruction Set

Table 9-1 divides the 80386 instruction set into classes and shows how the processor executes the instructions in each class in real and virtual 8086 modes. The instructions are grouped according to the 8086 family processor that introduced them.

A debugged 8086 binary program should not contain 80286 or 80386 instructions because such an instruction causes undefined behavior if executed by an 8086. Nevertheless, if such instructions are present in an 8086 program that is executed in real or V86 mode, they can

Table 9-1. Real and Virtual 8086 Mode Instruction Execution

Instruction Class	Real Mode	V86 Mode
8086 ADD, MOV, etc.	Executed	Executed
8086 PUSHF,POPF, INT,IRET,STI,CLI,Lock	Executed	IOPL-sensitive
8086 IN,OUT,INS,OUTS	Executed	I/O Map-sensitive
80286 ARPL, LSL, etc.	Opcode Fault	Opcode Fault
80286 LMSW, LIDT, etc.	Executed	GP Fault
80286 ENTER, BOUND, etc.	Executed	Executed
80386 32-bit extensions	Executed	Executed
80386 LFS, LGS, BT, SLD, etc.	Executed	Executed
80386 MOV CR0, MOV Dr, etc.	Executed	GP Fault

be executed, as shown in Table 9-1. Note that, as described in the next section, the 80386 32-bit instruction and operand addressing extensions (specified with 66H and 67H prefixes) can be executed in real and V86 modes, but are subject to 64 Kbyte limit checking. For example, an attempt to JMP or CALL to an offset greater than 64K results in a general protection exception, as does an attempt to address an operand located at an offset higher than 64K.

9.1.2 Pseudodescriptors

In real mode and V86 mode, as in protected mode, the 80386 uses the values in its descriptor registers to form and check linear addresses. When the descriptor registers are loaded with the values shown in Table 9-1, the 80386 mimics the logical-to-linear address translation of the 8086. However, descriptors do not exist in real mode and V86 mode; therefore, the contents of the descriptor registers in these modes are called pseudodescriptors. (Note also that no descriptor has the attributes listed in Table 9-2; for example, an 80386 segment cannot be both executable and writeable.) The processor initializes some pseudodescriptor values when it is reset (see Chapter 6), and loads others when it switches from protected mode to V86 mode. If the operating system switches the processor from protected mode to real mode, the operating system must first load pseudodescriptor values, as described in Section 9.2.

Software running in real mode or V86 mode can change the base address in a descriptor register. In these modes, the 80386 interprets a selector operand as a 16-bit address. When the processor loads a segment register in real mode or virtual 8086 mode, it shifts the selector value left by 4 and loads the resulting base address into the associated descriptor register. To compute a linear address, the 80386 adds an offset to the base address as usual; the resulting linear address is identical to the physical address that an 8086 computes by shifting a segment register value left by 4 and adding the offset.

Table 9-2. Pseudodescriptor Attributes

Attribute	Value
Present	1 (Present)
Base Address	<FFFFFH (<1MB)
Limit	FFFFH (64KB)
Granularity	0 (Byte)
Privilege Level — V86	3
Privilege Level — Real	0
Expansion Direction	0 (Up)
Readable	1 (Readable)
Writeable	1 (Writeable)
Executable	1 (Executable)
CS Default Operand	0 (16 Bits)
SS Big	0 (Small)

The pseudodescriptor-based addressing used by the 80386 in real and virtual 8086 modes differs from 8086 addressing (but is identical to 80286 real mode addressing) at the one-megabyte 8086 address space boundary. The 8086 "wraps" physical addresses that exceed 1 megabyte (possible when a segment's base is within the top 64K of the 8086 physical address space); the physical address following FFFFFH is effectively 0. Under the same conditions, the 80386, running in real or V86 mode, generates the linear address. (The highest linear address in real or virtual 8086 modes is 10FFEFH, the result of adding the maximum offset of FFFFH to the maximum base address of FFFFH shifted left 4 bits.) 8086 one-megabyte wraparound can be simulated in V86 mode with paging (see Section 9.3.3).

9.2 REAL MODE

The 80386 enters real mode when it is reset; operating system software can also switch the 80386 from protected mode to real mode. The differences between 80386 real mode and a true 8086 are documented in the *80386 Programmer's Reference Manual*. The differences are minor, and most 8086 application code runs without change in 80386 real mode. 80386 real mode is almost identical to 80286 real mode; consequently, 8086 binaries that execute correctly on a real mode 80286 are very likely to execute correctly on a real mode 80386 (the *80386 Programmer's Reference Manual* also describes the differences between 80286 and 80386 real modes).

Chapter 6 describes the values the 80386 registers contain following a hardware RESET, and how an operating system's initialization routine can switch the 80386 from real mode to protected mode. An operating system can also switch the 80386 from protected mode to real mode without resetting the chip. The assembly language code shown in Figure 9-1 illustrates the sequence of operations that switches the 80386 from protected mode to real mode.

When the 80386 is switched to real mode, the CS descriptor register must contain values that are 8086-compatible. Therefore, the operating system code that performs the switch must reside in a code segment whose descriptor has 8086-compatible attributes: present=1, privilege level=0, limit=64K, granularity=0, default operand size=0, conforming=0, and readable=1. If paging is enabled, the code and data segments used to make the switch must have physical addresses that are identical to their linear addresses (that is, the PTEs that map these segments must define an identity mapping). The identity mapping insures that instructions and operands are fetched from consistent physical addresses before and after paging is disabled.

Because, except for base address, descriptor register values cannot be loaded in real mode, 8086-compatible attributes must be loaded into the data segment descriptor registers before switching to real mode. To load these values, the operating system can define a data segment descriptor that contains 8086-compatible attributes (present=1, writeable=1, expansion direction=0, limit=64K, granularity=0, Big=0), and load a selector for this descriptor into SS, DS, ES, FS, and GS.

If paging is enabled, it must be disabled before entering real mode. This is done by clearing the PG bit in CR0; the next instruction must flush the TLB by moving any value to CR3. The 80386 is switched to real mode by clearing the PE bit in CRO. Immediately after the switch, the operating system must execute a JMP instruction to flush any instructions in the

```
;  THIS CODE HAS NOT BEEN TESTED
;  load data descriptor regs with values for real mode:
;    load=64K, present, writeable, expand-up, byte
;    granularity. New base address(es) must allow access to
;    this routine's data and stack.
         MOV      AX,RealModeSel   ; selector for descriptor
                                   ;   with real mode attributes
       MOV      DS,AX
       MOV      ES,AX
       MOV      SS,AX
       MOV      FS,AX
       MOV      GS,AX
;  prevent maskable interrupts while changing modes
         CLI
;  turn off paging
       MOV      EAX,CR0          ; get current CR0
       AND      EAX,7FFFFFFEH    ; turn off PG and PE bits
       MOV      CR0,EAX          ; disable paging, protection
       MOV      CR3,EAX          ; flush TLB by loading any value
;  turn off protection
       JMP      FlushQ           ; flush prefetch queue
FlushQ:                          ; now in real mode
;  set up real mode interrupt table; can be at any address
       MOV      AX,IntTabBase
       MOV      DS,AX
       LIDT     IntTabOffset     ; address of real mode int tbl
       STI                       ; interrupts on again
;  load 8086 program base addresses into data descriptor regs
       MOV      AX,1000H         ; 1000H is just an example
       MOV      DS,AX
       MOV      ES,AX
       MOV      SS,AX
       MOV      FS,AX
       MOV      GS,AX
;  load CS with real mode attributes and jump to 8086 program
       JMP      far ptr Entry86
```

Figure 9-1. Switching to Real Mode

80386 prefetch queue; such instructions have been decoded in protected mode and can be executed incorrectly in real mode.

The operating system must load IDTR with the address of the 8086 interrupt vector table. (The 80386 LIDT instruction works in real mode.) Unlike the 8086, the 80386 allows the interrupt vector table to reside at any linear address. Interrupts can be enabled after the real mode interrupt vector table has been established.

The base address values of the data descriptor registers can be loaded in the same way they are loaded in an 8086 program. Finally, the operating system can issue an intersegment JMP to the 8086 code. When executed in real mode, an intersegment JMP instruction loads the CS descriptor register with real mode attributes.

Nonmaskable interrupts can complicate switching to real mode because it is impossible to switch to real mode and switch to an 8086 interrupt vector table simultaneously. There is always an instant when the processor is in one mode but IDTR points to an interrupt table that has the format of the other mode. Systems that have supporting external hardware should disable nonmaskable interrupts, just as they disable maskable interrupts, during the switch. If nonmaskable interrupts cannot be disabled, the IDT must be overwritten with an 8086-format interrupt vector at offset 8 (the offset of the 8086 NMI interrupt vector). The 4-byte vector must be written with a single 32-bit MOV instruction (use 66H prefix), and the vector must be written after nonmaskable interrupts have been disabled and before switching to real mode. The 8086 vector at offset 8 of the IDT permits the processor to vector a nonmaskable interrupt through the protected mode IDT, should such an interrupt occur after real mode has been entered, but before the real mode interrupt table has been established.

9.3 VIRTUAL 8086 MODE

An 8086 application typically runs in a single task unprotected environment. The 8086 does not constrain the application in any way; it can issue all instructions and access all of memory. In the multitask protected mode environment of the 80386, only the operating system can issue all instructions and access all of memory; application code is usually constrained to addressing a subset of the address space and to executing a subset of the instruction set. Using virtual 8086 mode, an operating system can integrate an existing 8086 program into the protected, multitask (and optionally paged) environment of the 80386. The key attributes of a V86 task are summarized below and are described in more detail in the rest of this section:

*   The VM bit (in EFLAGS) of a V86 task is 1.

*   A V86 task runs at privilege level 3 when executing 8086 instructions; interrupts and exceptions switch the processor from V86 mode to protected mode and from privilege level 3 to privilege level 0; IRET instructions return the processor to V86 mode and privilege level 3.

*   A V86 task can execute concurrently with protected mode (VM=0) 80386 tasks, other V86 tasks, and 80286 tasks.

*   V86 tasks are compatible with paging and with virtual memory.

*   A V86 task can be allowed to reference memory-mapped and I/O-mapped devices, or these references can be trapped and simulated by the 80386 operating system.

*   A V86 task can be allowed to access the 80386 interrupt enable flag (IF), or references to IF can be trapped and simulated by the operating system.

9.3.1 Virtual Machine Monitors

Because their programs were written for a different machine and a different operating system, V86 tasks incur exceptions that the 80386 operating system must handle specially. For example, suppose a protected mode task issues an INT 21H instruction. Such an instruction is likely to be erroneous and cause for termination of the task. However, the same instruction issued by a V86 mode task might represent a legitimate 8086 operating system call.

It is convenient to package the code that responds specially to V86 exceptions in a procedure (or collection of procedures) called a virtual machine monitor (VMM). A VMM simulates the 8086 instructions that the 80386 will not execute in V86 mode. The virtual machine monitor's code must be contained in a 32-bit code segment whose DPL is 0. As Figure 9-2 shows, the VMM is called by an exception handler when the exception occurs in the context of a V86 task. To identify a V86 task, an exception handler can examine the VM bit in the EFLAGS image the 80386 saves on the handler's stack (Section 9.3.4 describes the format of a handler's stack when it is invoked in a V86 task).

To simulate an 8086 instruction, the VMM must locate and decode the instruction. The CS and EIP fields pushed onto the exception handler's stack contain the logical address of the faulting instruction. After simulating an instruction, the VMM must increment the EIP value on the stack so the V86 task will execute the following instruction when the exception handler returns. Note that a VMM should simulate only 8086 instructions; if an erroneous V86 task issues a privileged 80386 instruction, such as LGDT, the VMM should terminate the task.

9.3.2 Task Management

An 80386 operating system can create a V86 task directly, or it can create a protected mode task that transforms itself to a V86 task. To create a task that begins execution in virtual 8086 mode, an 80386 TSS must be initialized as follows:

- Set the EFLAGS VM bit to 1.

- Set the CS selector field so that when shifted left by 4, the result is the linear base address of the task's initial code segment.

- Set the IP field to the task's entry point.

- Set IOPL (in the EFLAGS field) to 3 if the task is to be able to access the interrupt enable flag; otherwise, set IOPL to 0 (see Section 9.3.4).

- Set the LDT selector field to 0 (null). (LDTs are not used in V86 mode; however, if an interrupt or exception procedure uses an LDT, the task's LDT selector must be initialized with a non-null selector.)

- Initialize the I/O permission map to grant or deny access to I/O ports (see Section 9.3.6); setting the permission map base field to FFFFH is equivalent to setting all permission bits (that is, to prohibiting all I/O space accesses).

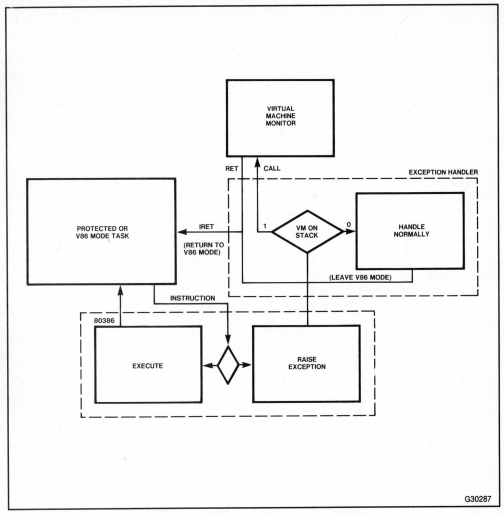

Figure 9-2. Invoking a Virtual Machine Monitor

In all other respects, V86 task creation is identical to protected mode task creation. When the TSS and other data structures used by the task are in place, the V86 task can be scheduled and dispatched like any protected mode task. When the V86 TSS is the new task in a task switch, the 80386 loads EFLAGS; because the VM bit is set, the 80386 switches to virtual 8086 mode. The processor interprets the remaining TSS fields as containing V86 values and loads them accordingly.

The second way to create a V86 task is to create a protected mode task that, running at privilege level 0, changes itself to a V86 task. To perform this transformation, the protected mode task must push a stack frame onto the level 0 stack that is identical to the frame pushed by the 80386 when a V86 task is interrupted or incurs an exception. Figure 9-4 shows

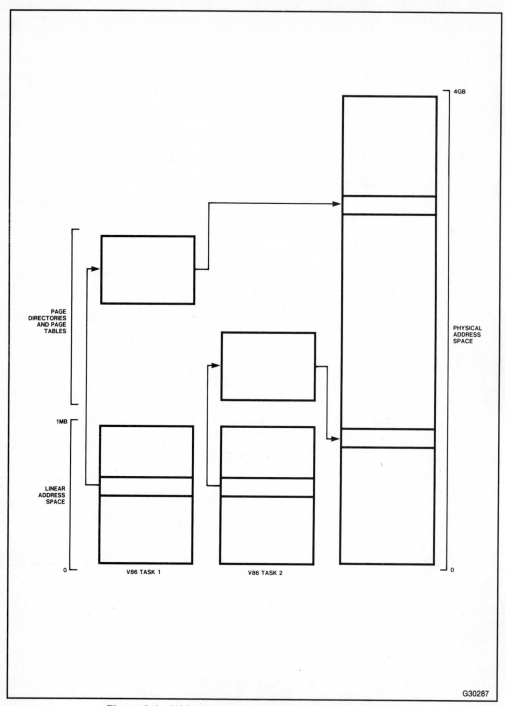

Figure 9-3. V86 Mode Address Relocation with Paging

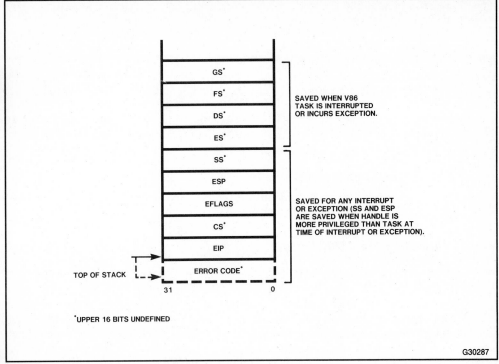

Figure 9-4. Handler's Stack after V86 Interrupt or Exception

the format of this stack frame. If the protected mode task then issues an IRET instruction, the 80386 loads the V86-format stack frame into its registers and continues execution in V86 mode. On the next task switch, the 80386 saves the V86 task's registers in V86 format.

9.3.3 Memory Management

Paging can be enabled as usual when virtual 8086 mode tasks are present. Indeed, if multiple V86 tasks can run concurrently, paging must be used to separate their physical address spaces; all V86 tasks run in the first megabyte of the linear space, as shown in Figure 9-3. With respect to paging, including page swapping, a V86 task is no different from a protected mode task; the guidelines provided in Chapter 2 apply to both kinds of tasks.

The 8086's 1-megabyte wraparound can be simulated with aliased pages. 256 page table entries are required to define a 1-megabyte physical address space and 16 more PTEs are required to define the 65,519 bytes above 1 megabyte that a V86 task can potentially address. By making the first 16 and the last 16 PTEs identical, any V86 reference to a linear address above 1 megabyte is relocated to the same physical address as a reference to the same displacement from linear address 0. In other words, the first and last 64 Kbytes of the linear space are mapped to the same physical pages. Note that as with all aliasing, this technique requires some extra operating system bookkeeping because multiple PTEs point to the same physical pages. For example, to swap out an aliased page, both PTEs that point to the page must be marked not-present.

9.3.4 Interrupts and Exceptions

In virtual 8086 mode, the processor treats interrupts and exceptions as it does when running in protected mode, except that it switches from V86 mode to protected mode before invoking a handler. When the handler issues an IRET instruction, the 80386 switches back to V86 mode and resumes execution of the V86 task. For the automatic V86-protected mode switching to operate properly, an operating system must observe the following:

*   All gates in the IDT must be 80386 gates.

*   Procedure-based handlers must reside in non-conforming privilege level 0 code segments; task-based handlers can run at any privilege level.

9.3.4.1 HANDLER CONSIDERATIONS

When a V86 task incurs an exception or is interrupted, the 80386 invokes the handler in a way that minimizes the difference between the V86 task and a protected mode task. If the interrupt or exception handler is a task, the 80386 switches to the handler task as usual, saving the V86 task's machine state in the old TSS. If the handler is a procedure, the 80386 first saves the V86 task's segment registers on the level 0 stack (see Figure 9-4), and then saves the usual EFLAGS, return address, and error code, as applicable to the interrupt or exception. (Pushing the additional segment registers slightly increases interrupt latency.) Because the top stack elements are identical when a handler is invoked in a protected mode task or in a V86 task, the handler can invariably return with an IRET instruction.

At entry to the handler, DS, ES, FS, and GS contain null selectors; SS and CS contain valid selectors as usual. If the handler needs to use DS-GS, it can push the segment registers in its prolog and pop them in its epilog without regard for the mode of the running task. When the handler issues an IRET instruction, the 80386 pops EIP, CS, EFLAGS, ESP, and SS from the handler's stack into the corresponding registers. When, after popping EFLAGS, the processor's VM bit is set, the processor additionally pops DS-GS from the stack.

The presence of V86 tasks is generally transparent to procedure-based interrupt and exception handlers. However, as mentioned earlier in Section 9.3.1, some exception handlers must examine the VM bit on the stack and call the virtual machine monitor if VM is set. Note also that interrupt or exception handlers that alter the running task's DS, ES, FS, or GS registers cannot do so directly if the running task is a V86 task; instead they must alter the register values on the level 0 stack.

9.3.4.2 INTERRUPT ENABLE FLAG CONSIDERATIONS

Some 8086 programs disable interrupts while they perform critical operations. An 80386 operating system can allow a V86 task to change IF or the operating system can direct the processor to raise a general protection exception if the task attempts to load or store IF. A V86 task runs at privilege level 3; its ability to access IF is determined by its IOPL. If a

V86 task's IOPL is less than 3, instructions that load or store IF result in general protection exceptions; the virtual machine monitor can simulate these instructions. If a V86 task's IOPL is equal to 3, the 80386 executes IF-related instructions. Because of the potential risk to the rest of the system, in general, a V86 task's IOPL should be set to 3 only when performance requirements cannot be met by simulating IF.

If a V86 task is denied direct access to IF, the VMM must simulate the following instructions: PUSHF, POPF, INT *n*, IRET, STI, and CLI. The VMM can maintain a variable (perhaps in the software portion of the task's TSS) that represents the task's simulated IF, supplying the variable's value to simulate instructions that store IF (for example, PUSHF) and updating the variable to simulate instructions that load IF (STI, for example).

Systems that permit V86 tasks to alter IF can deploy a hardware watchdog timer that generates a nonmaskable interrupt if a V86 task disables interrupts for too long. The watchdog timer can be implemented in coordination with the customary system timer that regularly interrupts on the INTR pin. Whenever the system timer interrupts, the operating system can load the watchdog timer with the value it loads into the system timer plus the maximum time interrupts are permitted to be disabled. As long as the system timer interrupts on schedule, the watchdog does not interrupt. If interrupts are disabled too long, however, the watchdog timer generates a nonmaskable interrupt, allowing the operating system to enable interrupts and terminate the V86 task.

Note that a V86 task whose IOPL is 3 can potentially issue any of the 256 INT instructions. To prevent such a V86 task from invoking an interrupt or exception handler with an INT *n* instruction, set the DPL field in the handler's IDT gate to 0. An attempt to invoke a handler through a gate whose DPL is 0 will result in a general protection exception; the VMM can then terminate the V86 task. If an IDT gate's DPL must be set to 3 to allow protected mode tasks running at privilege level 3 to invoke the associated handler, the handler can identify an erroneous V86 task by examining the VM bit on its stack. The handler can then call the virtual machine monitor which can terminate the V86 task.

9.3.4.3 SIMULATING INTERRUPTS

An 80386 operating system can deliver simulated interrupts to a V86 task. The technique is identical to reflecting a system call, described in Section 9.3.5. In essence, the virtual machine monitor builds a stack frame whose return address is the entry point of the V86 interrupt handler, and then issues an IRET instruction.

9.3.5 System Calls

Many 8086 operating systems use an INT *n* instruction for a system call. A V86 task's ability to execute an INT *n* instruction depends on the task's IOPL. If the V86 task's IOPL is less than 3, an INT *n* instruction results in a general protection exception. Invoked by the general protection exception handler, the VMM can handle the 8086 system call in one of two ways: it can simulate the call by making an equivalent call on the 80386 operating system, or it can reflect the call to a copy of the 8086 operating system loaded into the V86 task's address space (see Figure 9-5, which, for simplicity, omits the exception handler that calls the VMM). If a V86 task's IOPL is 3, it can issue an INT *n* instruction, which will

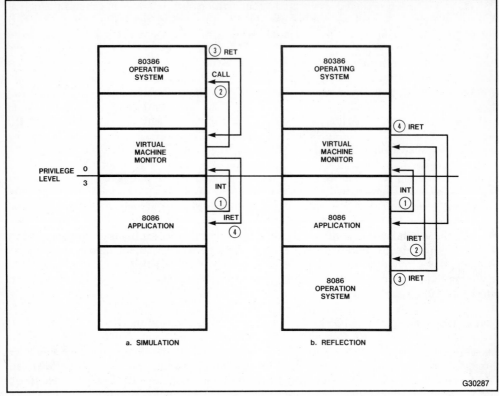

Figure 9-5. Simulating and Reflecting V86 System Calls

invoke the 80386 handler pointed to by gate *n* in the IDT. This handler can call the virtual machine monitor which can simulate or reflect the system call.

To simulate an 8086 system call, the VMM must decode the call, transform the call and the parameters to 80386 operating system equivalents, and call the 80386 operating system. When the 80386 operating system returns to the VMM, the VMM must transform the results into the format expected by the V86 task, advance the V86's task's saved EIP, and return to the V86 task with an IRET instruction.

If V86 system calls are to be handled by a copy of the 8086 operating system, the 8086 operating system must be allowed to initialize itself before any application code is executed. One way to do this is to load the 8086 operating system and let the 8086 operating system load the application. The 80386 operating system may need to invoke the 8086 operating system (using an IRET instruction) at an entry point other than its RESET address to avoid low-level hardware-dependent operations that can raise unnecessary exceptions if executed by a V86 task. Having initialized itself, a typical 8086 operating system can then wait for a command from an end-user. When a command requires loading an application, the 8086 operating system can do it.

Assuming an 8086 operating system and an 8086 application program reside together in a V86 task's address space, the virtual machine monitor can reflect a system call to the 8086 operating system as follows:

- Push a copy of the V86 task's stack frame (its segment registers, stack pointer, EFLAGS, and return address) onto the level 0 stack.

- Change the return address in the copied frame to the 8086 operating system's entry point (for an INT n system call, the address is located at linear address 4*n, that is, in the nth slot of the 8086 interrupt vector table).

- Simulate the 8086 INT instruction's push of the V86 task's FLAGS, CS, and IP onto the level 3 stack; adjust ESP in the copied stack frame on the level 0 stack to reflect the simulated push.

- Issue an IRET instruction to switch to virtual 8086 mode and transfer to the 8086 operating system's system call entry point.

When the 8086 operating issues an 8086 IRET instruction to return to the 8086 application, the VMM is invoked again. The VMM can return control to the 8086 application as follows:

- Adjust ESP to point to the original stack frame return address.

- Simulate the 8086 IRET instruction by copying FLAGS, CS and IP from the level 3 stack to their corresponding locations in the original stack frame (ESP in the original stack frame is correct as is).

- Increment EIP on the level 0 stack so it points to the instruction after the INT n instruction.

- Return to the exception handler which should return to the V86 task with an IRET instruction.

When paging is enabled, multiple V86 tasks can run concurrently, and a single copy of a reentrant 8086 operating system can be mapped into the address spaces of all V86 tasks. If the 8086 operating system is not reentrant, each V86 task must have its own copy of the 8086 operating system data; a single copy of the operating system code can be shared among the V86 tasks (unless the operating system modifies its code). Note that existence of multiple copies of an 8086 operating system necessitates coordinating their accesses to shared I/O devices (each copy of the 8086 operating system probably assumes it has exclusive access to all I/O devices). Section 9.3.6 describes how the virtual machine monitor can gain control when any of the 8086 operating systems attempts to access an I/O device.

9.3.6 Input/Output

A V86 task addresses a memory-mapped I/O device just as if it were running on an 8086. If paging is enabled, V86 task references to memory-mapped devices can be relocated automatically. For example, an 80386-based system may have a memory-mapped video refresh buffer located at a physical address higher than 1 megabyte. A similar buffer on an 8086-based system must necessarily be located below the 8086's 1-megabyte physical address limit. An 80386 operating system can initialize a V86 task's page tables so that its references to the addresses of the 8086-based buffer are automatically translated to the addresses of the 80386 buffer. Because this technique relocates all addresses in a page, it is best-suited to devices aligned on 4 Kbyte boundaries.

By clearing bits in a V86 task's I/O permission map, an 80386 operating system can permit the task to access selected I/O ports directly. (Chapter 5 describes the format and operation of the I/O permission map.) Note that, unlike a protected mode task, a V86 task's IOPL is irrelevant to the task's ability to access I/O ports; the 80386 examines only the I/O permission bits to determine V86 I/O port accessibility.

The accesses of multiple V86 tasks to the same I/O ports (whether memory- or I/O-mapped) must be serialized. Unless all V86 tasks perform I/O via a single copy of an 8086 operating system which performs the serialization, the serialization must be provided by the VMM. To insure that the VMM is invoked by any V86 I/O operation, I/O operations must be made to raise exceptions. Setting bits in the V86 task's I/O permission map makes references to the corresponding ports raise exceptions. References to memory-mapped devices can be made to raise exceptions by marking the associated pages not-present and setting an available PTE bit to indicate "trap on I/O." The page fault handler is invoked on a reference to a not-present page; if the page's trap on I/O bit is set, the page fault handler can invoke the VMM.

A UNIX System Implementation 10

CHAPTER 10
A UNIX SYSTEM IMPLEMENTATION

This chapter describes a hypothetical implementation of the UNIX System V kernel on the 80386. For convenience, we call this implementation U/386, but it corresponds to no actual system. The chapter will be of interest to readers who

- Want to see the 80386 system architecture applied to a complete operating system example
- Are porting the UNIX system to 80386-based hardware
- Are evaluating the 80386 as a "System V engine"

To get the most from this chapter, you should be moderately familiar with the UNIX System V kernel.

Only about 10 percent of the System V kernel is written in assembly language. These assembly language routines provide an interface between the processor and the bulk of the kernel, which is written in C. This chapter concentrates on the assembly language portions of the kernel because these are the routines that interact directly with the 80386 system architecture. The topics covered in this chapter are the lower levels of process management, memory management, system calls, interrupt and exception handling, I/O, and debug support.

Note that the UNIX System V is a proprietary product of AT&T. This chapter covers only subjects whose operation is common knowledge.

10.1 U/386 IMPLEMENTATION PHILOSOPHY

When implementing an existing operating system you must adapt one architecture to another. Either the operating system architecture must be adapted to the processor or the processor architecture must be adapted to the operating system. U/386 bridges this "architectural gap" by adapting the 80386 to the System V system architecture. Such an approach does not use every architectural feature of the 80386. However, tailoring the processor architecture to the operating system illustrates the flexibility of the 80386 system architecture, and shows how an existing operating system can be ported to the 80386 at minimum cost and risk. This chapter illustrates but one way to implement the System V system on the 80386; other design approaches can also be justified.

10.2 PROCESS AND MEMORY OVERVIEW

The traditional System V process-memory model is simple, although it has recently been made more elaborate to support greater interprocess sharing. (A System V process is analogous to an 80386 task and U/386 stores the machine state of process in a TSS.) In general, each process runs in its own address space, protected from all other processes.

The System V operating system distinguishes between user processes and system processes. Most processes are user processes; system processes typically perform housekeeping activities such as swapping out pages. A user process executing its own code is said to be running in user mode. A user mode process enters kernel mode as a result of a system call, an interrupt, or an exception. In kernel mode, a process executes kernel code, which can include privileged instructions. The kernel's code and data are mapped into each process's address space, but they are not directly accessible; a user process can do nothing to the kernel but call it. Conversely, the kernel has access to the running process's entire address space, which simplifies I/O transfers.

A process's address space is divided into functional areas called the text, data, and stack segments. However, from an addressing standpoint, the System V process address space is not segmented but uniform. For example, C programs routinely use the same pointer to alternately refer to an item on the stack and an item in the data segment. Although less common, some System V programs modify their own code or execute code that they generate on their stacks or in their data segments. Thus, System V segment types are not as distinct from one another as 80386 segment types. Although it is possible to map System V segments to 80386 segments, it is simpler to map them into what amounts to a single large 80386 segment that is subdivided into pages; this is the approach taken by U/386.

Figure 10-1 shows the 80386 linear address space during normal U/386 execution. A U/386 process uses one 80386 code and one data segment when it runs in user mode; it uses a different code segment and a different data segment when it runs in kernel mode. DS, ES, and SS are always loaded with the same descriptor. (U/386 uses ES for string instructions and does not use FS and GS.) The user segments begin at linear address 0 and extend over nearly the entire linear address space to the kernel boundary. U/386's segment arrangement gives each user process an unsegmented logical address space nearly 4 gigabytes long. In this flat address space, a pointer is simply a 32-bit offset, whether it points to code, a constant, or an item on the stack, because all segment base addresses are zero. Offset-only pointers match the C language's uniform view of the address space. Because a process's code is contained in a single code segment, function calls can be implemented with the fast intra-segment (near) CALL instruction.

The kernel's segments overlap the user's and extend to the 4 Gbyte limit of the linear address space. The kernel's segments have a privilege level of 0; the user segments are privilege level 3. Running at privilege level 0, the kernel can execute privileged instructions and is protected from the user. U/386 system calls, interrupts, and exceptions enter the kernel through a call gate, interrupt gates, and trap gates, respectively. When control passes through these gates, the 80386 loads the CS and SS registers automatically; the kernel loads DS and ES to gain access to its extended data segment. Note that by making the kernel's segments extended versions of the user's, a 32-bit pointer passed from user to kernel always points to the same linear address. U/386's segment arrangement also gives the kernel instant access to the user address space.

(A different design could extend the user segments to the full 4 gigabytes and protect the kernel's upper 4 megabytes of the linear space with page attributes. U/386 separates kernel from user by segmentation rather than paging because it is natural to define the division in the logical rather than the linear address space. However, both approaches are workable.)

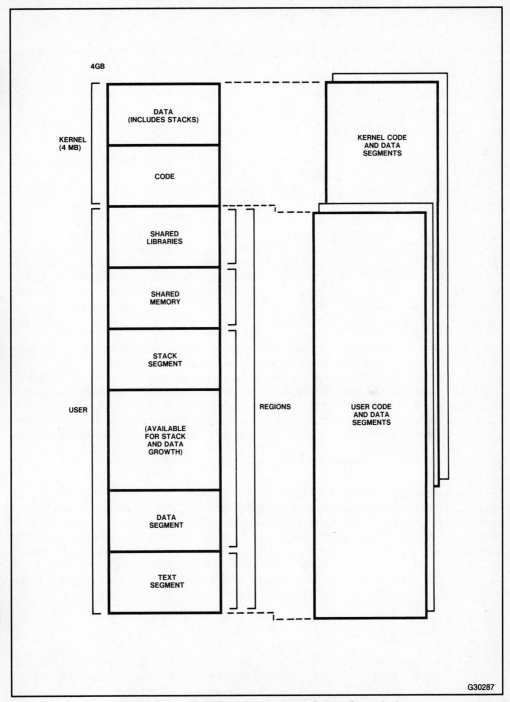

Figure 10-1. U/386 Linear Address Space Snapshot

Although U/386 uses 80386 segments lightly, it uses paging extensively to

- Sparsely allocate pages of physical memory to segments
- Protect processes from each other by mapping them to different pages of the 80386 physical address space
- Share memory between processes
- Implement demand paged virtual memory
- Protect a process from some of its own errors

Although a U/386 process can be almost as large as 4 gigabytes, most System V processes require only a fraction of the available space. To accommodate smaller processes efficiently, U/386 allocates only the number of pages a process actually uses. Although every process occupies nearly 4 Gbytes of the linear space, most processes occupy only tens or hundreds of pages of the physical space. The relocation provided by paging enables the kernel to give each process the impression that it is loaded beginning at linear address zero, whereas it is actually mapped to pages scattered over the physical address space. Although most of a process's pages are private to the process, U/386 processes can also share pages of code and data. U/386 implements virtual memory by swapping infrequently used pages out to disk when the supply of physical memory runs low, and swapping pages in from disk on demand. Finally, U/386 uses the protection attributes of pages to trap wild pointers and array indexes that fall into unallocated or read-only pages.

The notion of a *region* is central to System V memory management. A region is a sequence of consecutive logical addresses that the kernel can map into the user space of one or more processes. (Figure 10-1 shows that a process's System V segments are mapped to regions, and that regions are the basis for interprocess sharing.) In U/386, each active region is described in a kernel data structure called the region table. A region table entry points to the file, if any, associated with the region, and contains a field that identifies the region as public or private. A public region can be shared by other processes; a private region is private to a process. Public region table entries have a share count that indicates the number of processes whose address space currently includes the region.

U/386 implements a region as a list of page tables; because a page table covers 4 megabytes of memory, a typical region consists of a single page table. The kernel functions **attach** and **detach** map and unmap a public region into a process's address space. (This chapter uses a "special" typeface to distinguish System V terms.) The **attach** function increments a public region's share count and adds entries for the region's page table(s) to the process's page directory. The **detach** function invalidates the relevant page directory entries and decrements the share count; if the share count goes to zero (indicating the region is no longer attached to any process), **detach** frees the region.

10.3 PROCESSES

A System V process corresponds closely to an 80386 task. It is a unit of execution that runs in its own address space, executing (logically) in parallel with other processes. This section describes how U/386 represents, creates, and terminates processes. System V processes frequently execute the same program (for example, the **vi** editor or the C compiler), making program sharing an important aspect of an efficient implementation. Interprocess sharing is described in Section 10.4.5.

10.3.1 Representing a Process

A U/386 process is comanaged by the U/386 operating system and the 80386. Figure 10-2 shows the linked data structures that the operating system and the processor use to represent a process. The process table contains the minimal information the kernel needs to manage the active processes, principally each process's state and the address of its u s t r u c t (user structure). A u s t r u c t describes a process in detail; it contains the process's scheduling priority, accounting information, open file descriptors, kernel stack, and other machine-independent data. U/386 extends the u s t r u c t with the 80386's task management structure, the TSS. The complete one-page structure is called the u p a g e and contains essentially all process information.

A process's page directory and page tables are memory management structures and are described in detail in Section 10.4.2. Briefly, every page directory includes a common entry that maps the kernel's page table so that every process shares the kernel's pages. Other page directory entries map the page tables that implement the process's regions. Typically, one page table is sufficient to represent a region because a page table covers 4 megabytes. Not shown in Figure 10-2 are the GDT, which is shared by all processes and is described in Section 10.4.1.

Figure 10-3 shows the details of a U/386 process's TSS. (The TSS has been extended by a save area for the 80386 debug registers; Section 10.9 describes how this area is used.) U/386 does not use the back link field of the TSS, although the 80386 sets this field when it invokes a task-based exception handler. ESP0 points to the base of the kernel stack in the process's u s t r u c t; SS0 is a selector for the kernel data descriptor (described in Section 10.4.1). The remaining privileged stack pointers are not used because U/386 does not use privilege levels 1 and 2. The CR3 field contains the physical address of the process's page directory. The ES, SS, and DS fields contain selectors for the process's data segment; the CS field holds the selector for the process's code segment. The F and G segment registers are not used in U/386, so the corresponding TSS fields contain null selectors. The LDT field contains 0 because U/386 tasks do not have local segments; note that their distinct page directories prevent tasks from accessing each other's (unshared) physical memory, even though they generate the same linear addresses. Because U/386 user processes are not permitted to operate on I/O ports, their TSSs have null I/O guard maps.

10.3.2 Forking a Child Process

A System V process clones itself by issuing a f o r k system call. U/386 implements a f o r k system call as follows:

- Allocates a page for the new (child) process's u p a g e.
- Finds a free GDT slot for new process's TSS descriptor; initializes the descriptor to point to the TSS area of the new u p a g e.
- Copies the running (parent) process's u p a g e to the child's u p a g e.

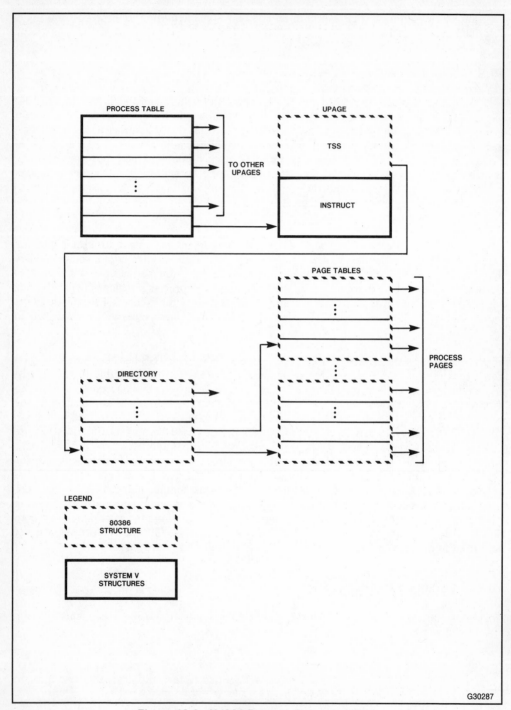

Figure 10-2. U/386 Process Representation

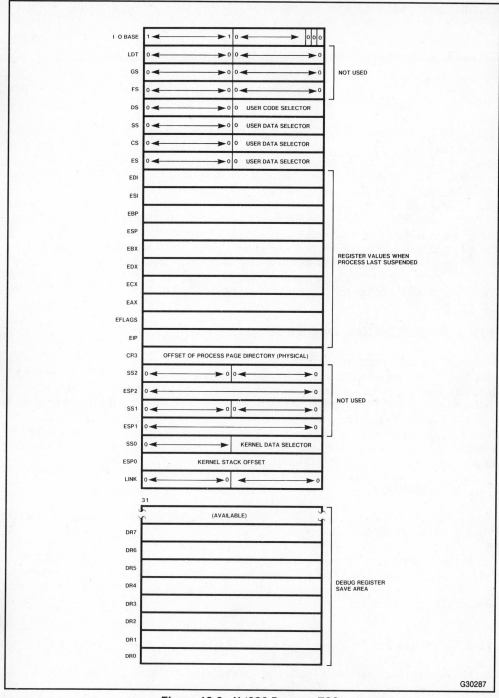

Figure 10-3. U/386 Process TSS

- Allocates a page for the child's page directory and loads the CR3 field in the child's TSS with the page directory's physical address.

- Attaches the parent's code, shared library, and shared memory regions to the child's address space. (Sharing these regions saves copying them from parent to child.)

- Creates a private region for the child's data region, but does not allocate the region's pages. Instead, U/386 copies the parent's data region page table(s) to the child, then marks both parent's and child's PTEs read-only and copy-on-write (explained below).

After a fork, the child has inherited its parent's regions, except the data region. Sharing these regions between parent and child causes no problems because the code and shared library regions are read-only; the shared memory region is by definition shared. The child must have its own data region, however, so it can write into the region without disturbing its parent. However, allocating pages for the child's data region is usually wasteful because most children quickly execute (by calling exec) a different program. By marking the parent's and the child's data region pages read-only, copy-on-write (one of the three available PTE bits is used to denote copy-on-write), U/386 defers allocation of data pages until the parent or the child actually writes into them. If the child reads a data page, it reads its parent's page. If the child or the parent writes into a data page, the 80386 raises a page fault. Noting that the target page is marked copy-on-write, the page fault handler allocates a page for the child, copies the parent's page to the child's, and makes both PTEs writeable.

10.3.3 Executing a New Program

A System V process executes a different program by issuing an exec system call. This call detaches the process's regions and then scans the region table for a public text region with the same name as the new program. If the program is found, exec attaches the text region to the process. If the text region is not found, exec creates a region for the text and fills it with text from the file; the new region is marked public if the file indicates that the program is pure (does not modify its code). exec then finds the file containing the program and creates a private region large enough to hold the program's data. exec does not load the data pages from the file, however, but initializes the process's page tables so the data pages demand-page in as they are referenced. exec does not return to its caller, but to the program it has just loaded.

10.3.4 Process Switching

To change processes, a kernel function (typically sleep) or the interrupt dispatcher (explained in Section 10.6.1) calls a kernel function called switch. switch saves the machine context of the old process and loads the machine context of the new process with a single JMP TSS instruction.

10.3.5 Process Termination

A process terminates by calling the kernel's exit function. exit cleans up the process by closing open files, and so on. To release the process's user memory, exit calls detach for each of the process's regions. If the child's parent is waiting for the child to terminate,

e x i t awakens the parent; if the parent is not waiting, **e x i t** sends the parent a SIGCHLD signal so the parent will wait. (The kernel's **i n i t** process waits for children whose parents have predeceased them.) When it has finished, **e x i t** calls **s w i t c h**. When the terminated process's parent executes **w a i t**, **w a i t** deletes the child from the process table and frees its page directory, **u p a g e**, and other kernel resources assigned ot it.

10.4 MEMORY MANAGEMENT

U/386 uses a combination of segmentation and paging to implement a memory management scheme that neatly matches the System V design.

10.4.1 Descriptor Tables

Figure 10-4 shows the GDT that all U/386 processes share. This simple structure contains one code descriptor that describes the kernel's code segment and one data descriptor that describes the kernel's data, stack, and extra segments. (In kernel mode the DS, SS, and ES registers all select the same descriptor.) Table 10-1 gives the attributes of these descriptors.

The user segments are similarly described by a code descriptor and a data descriptor in the GDT. (U/386 processes do not use an LDT; the per-process page directory separates the physical address spaces of processes.) Except for privilege level and limit, the user code and data descriptors are identical to the kernel's (see Table 10-2). U/386's system call gate is located in the GDT; Section 10.5 gives the attributes of this gate. The remaining GDT entries are for TSS descriptors, one descriptor for each active U/386 process.

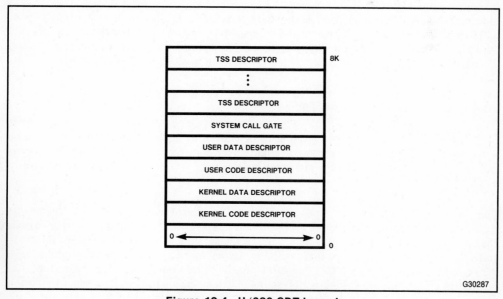

Figure 10-4. U/386 GDT Layout

Table 10-1. U/386 Kernel Segment Descriptors

Attribute	Code	Data
Base	0H	0H
Limit	0FFFFFH	0FFFFFH
Granularity	1B	1B
Default32/Big	1B	1B
Present	1B	1B
Privilege Level	00B	00B
Segment Descr.	1B	1B
Executable	1B	0B
Conform./Ex. Down	0B	0B
Read/Write	1B	1B

Table 10-2. U/386 User Segment Descriptors

Attribute	Code	Data
Base	0H	0H
Limit	0FF6FFH	0FF6FFH
Granularity	1B	1B
Default32/Big	1B	1B
Present	1B	1B
Privilege Level	11B	11B
Segment Descr.	1B	1B
Executable	1B	0B
Conform./Ex. Down	0B	0B
Read/Write	1B	1B

Figure 10-5 shows that all U/386 kernel data structures, whether defined by System V or the 80386, are effectively aliased by the kernel's data segment. This arrangement permits the kernel to update any of the 80386 system segments and tables (for example, TSSs and the GDT) without maintaining a separate data segment alias for each such segment or table.

10.4.2 Directories and Page Tables

Each U/386 process has its own page directory, allowing its physical address space to be separated from those of other processes. Figure 10-6 shows how a typical page directory is laid out. (This example shows a process whose regions are all less than 4 megabytes in length.)

The page directory entries correspond to System V regions (recall that U/386 implements regions with page tables). Although every process has a private data region, its other regions are (or may be, in the case of text) public. Thus, the kernel and shared library page directory entries are identical in all page directories; processes that execute the same program have the same text entry; and processes that attach to the same shared memory region share that entry as well (for simplicity, Figure 10-6 shows only a single shared memory region). Sharing page tables among processes is described in more detail in Section 10.4.5.

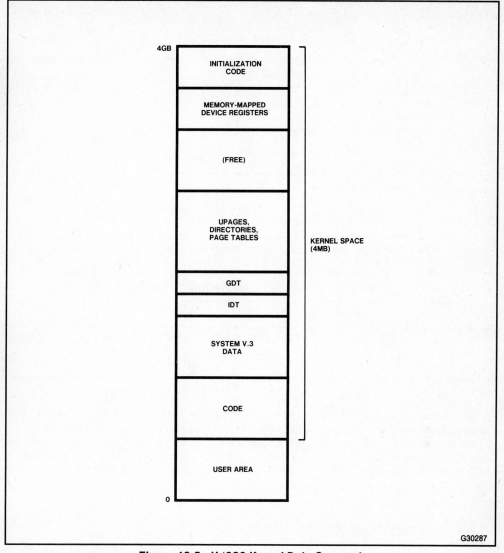

Figure 10-5. U/386 Kernel Data Segment

Table 10-3 shows how the entries in a page directory are encoded. The basic rules are

- All pages but the kernel's are accessible to the user. (Page-protecting the kernel's memory is technically redundant because it is already segment-protected.)

- All pages permit read-write access except for those containing code.

- The PDEs of all defined page tables are always marked present; pages are made not-present by changing their PTEs.

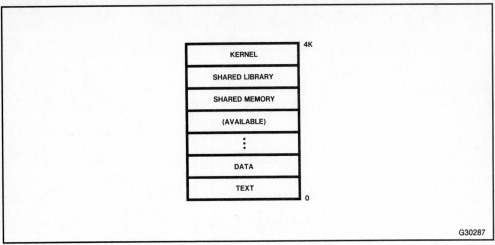

```
                                              4K
                    ┌──────────────────────┐
                    │        KERNEL         │
                    ├──────────────────────┤
                    │    SHARED LIBRARY     │
                    ├──────────────────────┤
                    │    SHARED MEMORY      │
                    ├──────────────────────┤
                    │     (AVAILABLE)       │
                    ├──────────────────────┤
                    │          ⋮           │
                    ├──────────────────────┤
                    │         DATA          │
                    ├──────────────────────┤
                    │         TEXT          │
                    └──────────────────────┘
                                              0
```

G30287

Figure 10-6. Typical U/386 Process Page Directory

Table 10-3. U/386 Page Directory Entry Attributes

Attribute	Kernel	ShLib.	ShMem.	Data	Text
User/Super.	0B	1B	1B	1B	1B
Read/Write	1B	0B	1B	1B	0B
Present	1B	1B	1B	1B	1B

Process page table entries have the same attributes as their page directory entries (for example, text pages are read-only), except that the present bit changes dynamically as the virtual memory subsystem moves pages between memory and disk. Because processes share several page tables, the U/386 per-process page table overhead is minimal. A new process requires only a data page table if it shares text with another process, or a data and a text page table if no other process is executing the same program.

10.4.3 Managing the Stack and the Heap

A U/386 process's stack and heap are located at opposite ends of its data region and grow toward each other as shown in Figure 10-7. The heap grows toward higher addresses as a result of explicit s b r k system calls. (The top of the heap is called the break and s b r k "sets the break.") The stack grows down automatically as a result of page faults.

When it creates a process, the kernel marks the pages between the initial top of the stack and the initial top of the heap as not-present, both to avoid allocating pages that are not in use, and to trap references to these unallocated pages. The page fault handler treats a reference to one of these not-present and unallocated pages as an implicit request to extend the stack. After checking that the referenced page is not below the break (that is, it has not been allocated to the heap), the page fault handler allocates the page and marks it present.

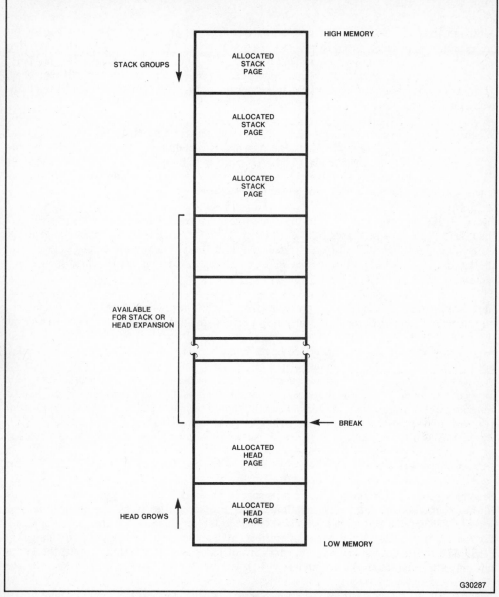

Figure 10-7. U/386 Stack and Heap Expansion

The heap grows up toward the stack by explicit calls to the kernel's s b r k system call. Such calls are typically made by language run-time routines such as m a l l o c in C. s b r k moves the break up by the number of bytes requested in the call, rounded up to the next page boundary. s b r k does not allocate the pages just added to the heap; the pages are allocated by the page fault handler when and if the pages are referenced.

10.4.4 Protection

Although it is mapped into the address space of every process, the kernel's memory is protected by its privilege level. Kernel segments are privilege level 0; user segments are privilege level 3. (Kernel pages also have supervisor privilege and user pages have user privilege, but this protection is redundant in U/386 because the 80386 checks segment privilege levels first.) User code has no direct access to kernel memory, only indirect access through the system call gate.

When the kernel creates a user process, it sets the process's IOPL to 0; this prevents the process from issuing I/O instructions except when it is running at privilege level 0 — that is, when it is executing kernel code. (The I/O guard map base field of U/386 TSSs is set to FFFFH, which effectively sets guard bits on all ports.) User code cannot issue 80386 privileged instructions because user code always runs at privilege level 3.

Every U/386 process is mapped to the same linear addresses because every process shares the GDT. To protect processes from each other, U/386 processes have separate page directories. Every process has a different set of pages in the physical address space, except for the kernel pages, which all processes share, and the shared regions described in the next section.

Separate page directories protect processes from each other, whereas page protection attributes protect a process from some of its own errors. If a process executes a pure program, the kernel marks the process's code pages read-only. Although a process's allocated data pages are marked read-write, the free pages lying between its stack and heap are marked not-present, allowing the processor to trap references to these pages caused by wild pointers or array indexes. Note that because a process's read-write data segment overlays its read-only code segment in the linear space, a program, such as an interpreter, can write instructions into its data segment and then execute them by jumping to the same address in its code segment. (The 80386 does not define writeable code segments.)

10.4.5 Sharing

System V processes run in separate address spaces, but in System V they can share programs, library routines, and data. Regions allow these diverse entities to be shared in a uniform way. U/386 implements regions with 80386 page tables. Page tables are convenient units for sharing because a shared page is described by a single page table entry. To change the attributes of a page, for example, to mark it not-present after swapping it out, the kernel has only one page table entry to update.

Besides sharing entire program texts (see Section 10.3.3), System V allows frequently used functions to be shared across programs. Such functions, which typically include standard I/O and string handling routines, are contained in shared libraries known to the linker. When the linker encounters a reference to a shared library function, it does not insert the function's code into the object file, but rather a special identifier. At initialization time, the kernel loads shared libraries into the public shared library region. As it loads a program, the kernel resolves object file references to shared libraries with addresses in the shared library region.

Processes can share data through System V's shared memory facility. U/386 implements shared memory as public regions (that is, as shared page tables). The kernel honors a process's request to attach shared memory by simply attaching the region like any other.

10.4.6 Virtual Memory

The U/386 kernel demand pages the user space but not the kernel space. Although this approach is typical of System V implementations, a more sophisticated design could page out at least part of the kernel, for example, the per-process u p a g es, page directories, and page tables.

U/386 virtual memory management consists of a system process called the pager and the page fault handler, which is implemented as a procedure. Figure 10-8 shows the format of the page table entries used by the pager and the page fault handler.

The locked bit identifies a page that should be immune from paging and swapping. The copy-on-write bit identifies a parent's data page that should not be copied to the child's address space until the child writes to the page. The disk block number of a swapped-out page is kept in the disk address field.

U/386 also defines a free frame list, which contains page frames that are available for allocation, and an allocated frame list which defines allocated page frames. U/386 always allocates from the front of the free frame list, but may place a newly freed frame on the front or the back. A frame goes on the front of the list if the data in the frame is of no further use (a frame from a terminated process's stack is an example). A frame containing data that may be needed again (for example, a text page from a process) is placed on the back of the list to delay its reallocation. Frames can be reclaimed quickly from the free list as described below.

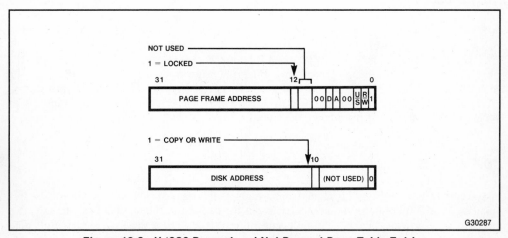

Figure 10-8. U/386 Present and Not-Present Page Table Entries

The kernel activates the pager process when the number of free frames reaches a "low water mark"; the pager runs until it builds the list up to a "high water mark." Ignoring locked pages, the pager cycles around the circular allocated frame list, examining each frame's accessed bit (that is, the accessed bit of the PTE that maps the frame). If the accessed bit is set, the page was used recently; the pager clears the bit and moves to the next allocated frame. If the accessed bit is clear, the page has not been used recently (that is, the page has not been accessed since the pager last cleared the page's accessed bit). Such a page is a good candidate to page out so its frame can be freed.

Having identified a page to remove from memory, the pager examines the page's dirty bit to determine if the page must be written to disk. If the dirty bit is set, the page has been updated since it was swapped-in and must be written to disk. If the dirty bit is clear, the disk copy of the page is current. (The page fault handler clears the dirty bit when it swaps-in a page.) If the page does not need to be written, the pager marks the page not-present and adds the page to the tail of the free list. Otherwise, the pager adds the page to a list of pages that must be written to disk. Another system process writes these pages and then frees their frames.

When a process attempts to access a not-present page, the 80386 invokes the page fault handler. The U/386 handler is implemented as a procedure that runs in the context of the faulting process. The page fault handler uses CR2 and CR3 to find the not-present page table entry that caused the fault. To retrieve the page, the handler first searches the free list for the page frame. If the handler finds the page on the free list, it reclaims the frame by removing it from the free list and adding it to the allocated list; it then marks the PTE present and accessed, and returns. If the frame is not on the free list, the page fault handler allocates a frame from the head of the free list and calls the page device driver to read the page into the frame. The handler puts it process to sleep until the page has been read. When awakened, the handler updates the page's PTE with its new frame address, marks the page present and accessed (so it will stay in memory for at least one pager cycle), and returns.

10.4.7 Locking

A System V process (running with super-user privilege) can prevent itself from being paged or swapped out by issuing the p l o c k system call. U/386 locks a process in memory by first setting a flag in the process's u p a g e to mark the process locked. This makes the process immune to swapping (process swapping, not page swapping). p l o c k then sets the lock bit in all of the process's present pages. Whenever the page fault handler brings in a page, it checks the process's lock bit in the u p a g e. If it is set, the pager marks the page's PTE locked to prevent it from being paged out.

10.5 SYSTEM CALLS

A typical UNIX system call is made from a high-level language such as C, and is ultimately handled by a C function in the kernel. Between the caller and the handler is some assembly langue that provides a language-independent interface across the user-kernel protection boundary. Figure 10-9 shows how this assembly language is implemented in U/386.

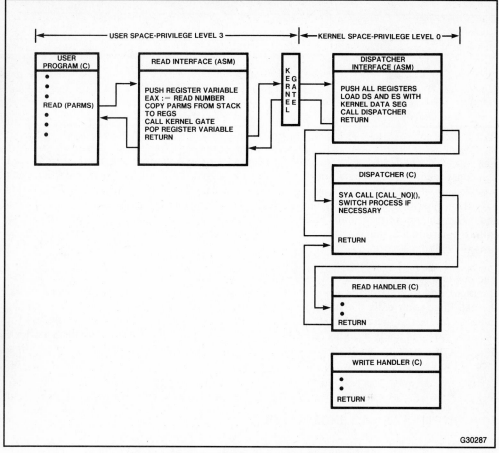

Figure 10-9. U/386 System Call Dispatching

U/386 follows the conventional System V practice of providing a single kernel entry point, implemented as an 80386 call gate. Table 10-4 shows the attributes of the U/386 system call gate.

In Figure 10-9, the two key routines are the system call interface (one for each system call) and the call dispatcher interface. The call interface is the function the linker provides to satisfy the user program's reference to a system call. Following normal C practice, at entry to the call interface, the parameters to be passed to the system function are on the stack. The call interface pushes any registers that contain C register variables. It then loads EAX with a number that identifies the system call to the call dispatcher. The call interface then copies parameters from the stack to registers and issues an intersegment CALL to the kernel's call gate. The call gate is initialized to copy 0 doublewords of parameters from the user's to the kernel's stack.

Table 10-4. U/386 Call Gate Attributes

Attribute	Value
Selector	(Kernel Code Descriptor in GDT)
Offset	(Dispatcher Interface)
Present	1B
Privilege Level	11B
Type	01100B
Dword Count	00000B

The intersegment CALL (whose selector operand is a call gate) instruction loads SS and CS; consequently, the process's privilege level is changed to 0, and the kernel uses the stack provided for it in the process's u p a g e. The dispatcher interface pushes all registers (this puts the system call parameters and the call number on the kernel's stack) and loads DS and ES with the kernel's data segment selector. Having established addressability and a calling environment that conforms to C's calling conventions, the call dispatcher interface calls the call dispatcher.

The machine-dependent transitions from the user's environment to the kernel's is now complete, and the rest of the system call is handled in C. Using the call number as an index, the call dispatcher calls the function in the kernel that handles the system call. When the function returns to the call dispatcher, the call dispatcher checks a flag to see if the call (or an interrupt) has made a higher priority process ready. If so, the dispatcher calls s w i t c h to switch processes rather than returning via the dispatcher interface and system call interface to the user code. The next time the process runs, control will return to the user by this route.

10.6 INTERRUPTS AND EXCEPTIONS

System V and the 80386 inevitably handle interrupts and exceptions somewhat differently. With a small amount of assembly language, however, the 80386 can be tailored to fit the System V model neatly, as described in this section.

10.6.1 Interrupts

System V dispatches interrupts in much the same way that it dispatches system calls. (Note that the system call dispatcher and the interrupt dispatcher distribute system calls and interrupts to their respective handlers; these dispatchers are distinct from the dispatcher that switches processes.) U/386 essentially provides an assembly language interface between the 8259A Programmable Interrupt Controller(s) and the System V interrupt dispatcher. Figure 10-10 shows this interface. Each interrupt source is associated with a different interrupt gate in the IDT. The interrupt gate points to a short device-specific piece of privilege level 0 code that saves the ID of the interrupting device on the kernel stack. (The interrupt gate is initialized so that an interrupt switches the 80386 to kernel mode just as a call through a call gate does.) All interrupts go through the remaining dispatcher interface code. The common code saves all registers on the kernel stack and resets the interrupt controller; exactly

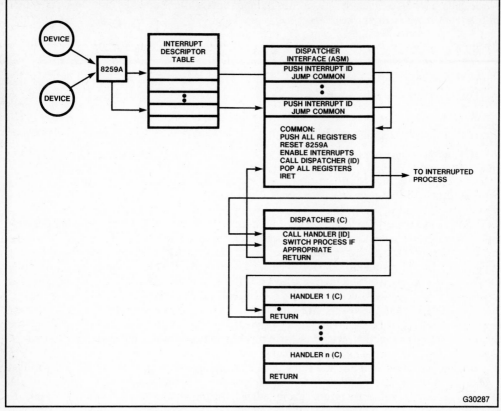

Figure 10-10. U/386 Interrupt Dispatching

what "resets" means depends on how many interrupt controllers the system uses and how they are programmed. Having made the interrupt controller able to pass along the next interrupt, the common code enables processor interrupts by issuing an STI instruction. It then calls the interrupt dispatcher, passing the interrupt ID as a parameter.

The interrupt dispatcher is a machine-independent C function that uses the interrupt ID as an index to the proper interrupt handler (also written in C). After the handler returns, the interrupt dispatcher switches to a new process if the current process was interrupted in user mode and if the handler awakened a higher-priority process.

10.6.2 Blocking Interrupts in the Kernel

System V defines a series of machine-independent kernel routines that set the kernel's priority level. Priority level 7 is high and is assigned to the clock; block and character devices have priority levels 6 and 5, respectively. Kernel routines, notably device drivers, call s p l *n* to return the current priority level and set the priority level to *n*. For example, a disk device driver calls ⊆ p l 6 to block out all but clock interrupts while it updates data structures that an interrupt handler might also use.

U/386 implements the ⊆ p l routines (in assembly language) as follows:

- Save current priority level
- Disable processor interrupts
- Reprogram interrupt controller(s) to block interrupts below new level
- Enable processor interrupts
- Return old priority level

10.6.3 Exceptions

As Table 10-5 shows, the U/386 kernel responds to an 80386 exception differently depending on whether the exception occurs in user or kernel mode. (The kernel disables interrupts and changes the IDT on entry to and exit from the kernel.) U/386 transforms most user mode exceptions into standard UNIX signals. (An exception handler sends a signal by calling the kernel's p ⊆ i g n a l function; p ⊆ i g n a l finds the addresses of the process's signal handlers, if any, in the process's u p a g e.) Exceptions that occur in the kernel generally indicate unrecoverable problems and should, except for hardware-related exceptions, never occur in a debugged kernel. The kernel responds to these fatal exceptions by calling the System V p a n i c function, which prints a message on the console and halts the system.

The double fault, invalid TSS, and stack fault exceptions occurring in the kernel are handled by exception tasks. The handlers for these exceptions cannot assume that the context of the faulting process is valid; therefore, the handlers are implemented as 80386 tasks and are represented in the IDT by task gates. When one of these exceptions occurs, the 80386 switches

Table 10-5. U/386 Kernel Exception Handling

Number	Name	User Action	Kernel Action
0	Divide Error	SIGILL	Panic
1	Single Step	SIGTRAP	Monitor
2	NMI	Panic	Panic
3	Breakpoint	SIGTRAP	Monitor
4	Overflow	SIGSEGV	Panic
5	Bounds	SIGSEGV	Panic
6	Invalid Opcode	SIGILL	Panic
7	No Coproc.	Emulate	Panic
8	Double Fault	Panic	Panic (task)
9	Coproc. Overrun	SIGSEGV	Panic
10	Invalid TSS	Panic	Panic (task)
11	Segment Fault	Panic	Panic
12	Stack Fault	SIGSEGV	Panic (task)
13	Protection	SIGSEGV	Panic
14	Page Fault	Get Page	Get Page
16	Coproc. Error	SIGFPE	Panic
other	(undefined)	SIGILL	Panic

to the interrupt task, which has a known-good context. Because these faults are fatal, no return occurs, so the task switch can be done by the 80386 without kernel involvement.

10.7 INPUT/OUTPUT

UNIX system device drivers are written in C and are largely processor-independent. U/386 support for device drivers consists of a few assembly language routines (in addition to the s p l routines described earlier) and a convention that provides drivers with the physical addresses of buffers.

U/386 supports memory-mapped and I/O-mapped devices. Drivers can address memory-mapped device registers directly; these devices are mapped into the top of the kernel data segment. To permit drivers to access the 80386 I/O space, the kernel provides a set of assembly language routines that transfer bytes, words, or dwords to or from I/O ports. These routines use the various forms of the IN and OUT instructions.

To move data between user areas and kernel buffers, U/386 supplies the c o p y i n and c o p y o u t routines. The heart of these assembly language routines is the MOVS (move string) instruction. Isolating MOVS in these two routines allows the kernel to determine whether a fault occurring in the execution of the instruction is caused by a user error or a kernel bug. A user may pass a bad address or count in a r e a d or w r i t e system call. If, when moving the data across the user/kernel boundary, a general protection fault occurs, the fault handler can determine if the offending instruction is in c o p y i n or c o p y o u t. If so, it knows the fault is a result of a user error, and it can send a signal to the user process. If the fault occurs in another routine, it indicates a kernel bug, so the fault handler calls p a n i c.

The standard System V block device interface transfers blocks between kernel buffers and devices. The DMA controllers incorporated in typical device controllers cannot read or write these buffers with logical addresses because they have no knowledge of the 80386 descriptor and page tables. U/386 enables drivers to supply physical addresses to DMA controllers as follows. During initialization, the kernel allocates a pool of I/O buffers that drivers use for block transfers. Each of these buffers has a header that the kernel initializes with the physical address of the actual buffer. When the kernel calls a driver to process an I/O request, it passes the driver the logical address of a buffer header. The driver can copy the physical address from the buffer header to the DMA controller without incurring any logical-to-physical translation overhead. The kernel breaks I/O requests that cross page boundaries into multiple requests.

10.8 NUMERICS

By default, U/386 lets the 80287 or 80387 numeric coprocessor (or emulator) handle the errors it discovers. However, nothing prevents an assembly language program from unmasking the errors so they can be handled by the program. Unmasked errors are delivered via standard floating point signal (SIGFPE). The program's signal handler can use the FSTENV instruction to find out what happened.

10.9 DEBUG SUPPORT

The System V p t r a c e system call allows a debugger to inspect and modify the representation of the child process it is debugging. The debugger runs such a program as a child and calls p t r a c e to set breakpoints, change registers, etc. By making the 80386 breakpoint registers accessible to p t r a c e, just like other registers, the debugger can gain access to the breakpoint registers.

U/386 debuggers use the INT 3 (1-byte interrupt) instruction to implement instruction breakpoints. (Because the kernel's data segment overlaps its text segment, a debugger running in kernel mode can overwrite code with the INT 3 instruction.) The four breakpoint registers are used to implement data breakpoints.

LITERATURE SALES FORM (EUROPE)

NAME: _____

COMPANY: _____

ADDRESS: _____

_____

_____

PHONE NO.: _____

ORDER NO.	TITLE	QTY.	PRICE	TOTAL
☐☐☐☐☐☐ – ☐☐☐	_____	___ × ___ = ___
☐☐☐☐☐☐ – ☐☐☐	_____	___ × ___ = ___
☐☐☐☐☐☐ – ☐☐☐	_____	___ × ___ = ___
☐☐☐☐☐☐ – ☐☐☐	_____	___ × ___ = ___
☐☐☐☐☐☐ – ☐☐☐	_____	___ × ___ = ___
☐☐☐☐☐☐ – ☐☐☐	_____	___ × ___ = ___
☐☐☐☐☐☐ – ☐☐☐	_____	___ × ___ = ___
☐☐☐☐☐☐ – ☐☐☐	_____	___ × ___ = ___
☐☐☐☐☐☐ – ☐☐☐	_____	___ × ___ = ___
☐☐☐☐☐☐ – ☐☐☐	_____	___ × ___ = ___
☐☐☐☐☐☐ – ☐☐☐	_____	___ × ___ = ___

Subtotal _____

Your Local Sales Tax _____

Postage _____

Total _____

PAYMENT

Cheques should be made payable to your local Intel Sales Office.

Other forms of payment may be available in your country. Please contact the Literature Coordinator at your local Intel Sales Office for details.

The Completed form should be marked for the attention of the LITERATURE CO-ORDINATOR and returned to your local Intel Sales Office.

DOMESTIC SALES OFFICES

ALABAMA

†Intel Corp.
5015 Bradford Dr., #2
Huntsville 35805
Tel: (205) 830-4010

ARIZONA

†Intel Corp.
11225 N. 28th Dr.
Suite D-214
Phoenix 85029
Tel: (602) 869-4980

Intel Corp.
1161 N. El Dorado Place
Suite 301
Tucson 85715
Tel: (602) 299-6815

CALIFORNIA

†Intel Corp.
21515 Vanowen Street
Suite 116
Canoga Park 91303
Tel: (818) 704-8500

†Intel Corp.
2250 E. Imperial Highway
Suite 218
El Segundo 90245
Tel: (213) 640-6040

Intel Corp.
1510 Arden Way, Suite 101
Sacramento 95815
Tel: (916) 920-8096

†Intel Corp.
4350 Executive Drive
Suite 105
San Diego 92121
Tel: (619) 452-5880

Intel Corp.*
400 N. Tustin Avenue
Suite 450
Santa Ana 92705
Tel: (714) 835-9642
TWX: 910-595-1114

†Intel Corp.*
San Tomas 4
2700 San Tomas Expressway
2nd Floor
Santa Clara, CA 95051
Tel: (408) 986-8086
TWX: 910-338-0255

COLORADO

Intel Corp.
4445 Northpark Drive
Suite 100
Colorado Springs 80907
Tel: (303) 594-6622

†Intel Corp.*
650 S. Cherry St., Suite 915
Denver 80222
Tel: (303) 321-8086
TWX: 910-931-2289

CONNECTICUT

†Intel Corp.
26 Mill Plain Road
2nd Floor
Danbury 06811
Tel: (203) 748-3130
TWX: 710-456-1199

FLORIDA

†Intel Corp.
242 N. Westmonte Dr.
Suite 105
Altamonte Springs 32714
Tel: (305) 869-5588
FAX: 305-682-6047

Intel Corp.
6363 N.W. 6th Way, Suite 100
Ft. Lauderdale 33309
Tel: (305) 771-0600
TWX: 510-956-9407
FAX: 305-772-8193

Intel Corp.
11300 4th Street North
Suite 170
St. Petersburg 33716
Tel: (813) 577-2413
FAX: 813-578-1607

GEORGIA

†Intel Corp.
3280 Pointe Parkway
Suite 200
Norcross 30092
Tel: (404) 449-0541

ILLINOIS

†Intel Corp.*
300 N. Martingale Road, Suite 400
Schaumburg 60173
Tel: (312) 310-8031

INDIANA

†Intel Corp.
8777 Purdue Road
Suite 125
Indianapolis 46268
Tel: (317) 875-0623

IOWA

Intel Corp.
1930 St. Andrews Drive N.E.
2nd Floor
Cedar Rapids 52402
Tel: (319) 393-5510

KANSAS

†Intel Corp.
8400 W. 110th Street
Suite 170
Overland Park 66210
Tel: (913) 345-2727

MARYLAND

†Intel Corp.*
7321 Parkway Drive South
Suite C
Hanover 21076
Tel: (301) 796-7500
TWX: 710-862-1944

Intel Corp.
7833 Walker Drive
Suite 550
Greenbelt 20770
Tel: (301) 441-1020

MASSACHUSETTS

†Intel Corp.*
Westford Corp. Center
3 Carlisle Road
2nd Floor
Westford 01886
Tel: (617) 692-3222
TWX: 710-343-6333

MICHIGAN

†Intel Corp.
7071 Orchard Lake Road
Suite 100
West Bloomfield 48322
Tel: (313) 851-8096

MINNESOTA

Intel Corp.
3500 W. 80th St., Suite 360
Bloomington 55431
Tel: (612) 835-6722
TWX: 910-576-2867

MISSOURI

Intel Corp.
4203 Earth City Expressway
Suite 131
Earth City 63045
Tel: (314) 291-1990

NEW JERSEY

Intel Corp.*
328 Newman Springs Road
Red Bank 07701
Tel: (201) 747-2233

Intel Corp.
75 Livingston Avenue
First Floor
Roseland 07068
Tel: (201) 740-0111

NEW MEXICO

Intel Corp.
8500 Menaul Boulevard N.E.
Suite B 295
Albuquerque 87112
Tel: (505) 292-8086

NEW YORK

Intel Corp.*
850 Cross Keys Office Park
Fairport 14450
Tel: (716) 425-2750
TWX: 510-253-7391

Intel Corp.*
300 Motor Parkway
Hauppauge 11787
Tel: (516) 231-3300
TWX: 510-227-6236

Intel Corp.
15 Myers Corner Road
Suite 2B
Wappingers Falls 12590
Tel: (914) 297-6161
TWX: 510-248-0060

NORTH CAROLINA

Intel Corp.
5700 Executive Drive
Suite 213
Charlotte 28212
Tel: (704) 568-8966

†Intel Corp.
2700 Wycliff Road
Suite 102
Raleigh 27607
Tel: (919) 781-8022

OHIO

Intel Corp.*
3401 Park Center Drive
Suite 220
Dayton 45414
Tel: (513) 890-5350
TWX: 810-450-2528

Intel Corp.*
25700 Science Park Dr., Suite 100
Beachwood 44122
Tel: (216) 464-2736
TWX: 810-427-9298

OKLAHOMA

Intel Corp.
6801 N. Broadway
Suite 115
Oklahoma City 73162
Tel: (405) 848-8086

OREGON

†Intel Corp.
15254 N.W. Greenbrier Parkway, Bldg. B
Beaverton 97006
Tel: (503) 645-8051
TWX: 910-467-8741

PENNSYLVANIA

Intel Corp.*
455 Pennsylvania Avenue
Suite 230
Fort Washington 19034
Tel: (215) 641-1000
TWX: 510-661-2077

Intel Corp.*
400 Penn Center Blvd., Suite 610
Pittsburgh 15235
Tel: (412) 823-4970

PUERTO RICO

Intel Microprocessor Corp.
South Industrial Park
P.O. Box 910
Las Piedras 00671
Tel: (809) 733-8616

TEXAS

†Intel Corp.
313 E. Anderson Lane
Suite 314
Austin 78752
Tel: (512) 454-3628

†Intel Corp.*
12300 Ford Road
Suite 380
Dallas 75234
Tel: (214) 241-8087
TWX: 910-860-5617

Intel Corp.*
7322 S.W. Freeway
Suite 1490
Houston 77074
Tel: (713) 988-8086
TWX: 910-881-2490

UTAH

Intel Corp.
5201 Green Street
Suite 290
Murray 84123
Tel: (801) 263-8051

VIRGINIA

†Intel Corp.
1504 Santa Rosa Road
Suite 108
Richmond 23288
Tel: (804) 282-5668

WASHINGTON

Intel Corp.
155 108th Avenue N.E.
Suite 386
Bellevue 98004
Tel: (206) 453-8086
TWX: 910-443-3002

Intel Corp.
408 N. Mullan Road
Suite 102
Spokane 99206
Tel: (509) 928-8086

WISCONSIN

†Intel Corp.
330 S. Executive Dr.
Suite 102
Brookfield 53005
Tel: (414) 784-8087
FAX: (414) 796-2115

CANADA

BRITISH COLUMBIA

Intel Semiconductor of Canada, Ltd.
4585 Canada Way, Suite 202
Burnaby V5G 4L6
Tel: (604) 298-0387
FAX: (604) 298-8234

ONTARIO

†Intel Semiconductor of Canada, Ltd.
2650 Queensview Drive
Suite 250
Ottawa K2B 8H6
Tel: (613) 829-9714
TLX: 053-4115

†Intel Semiconductor of Canada, Ltd.
190 Attwell Drive
Suite 500
Rexdale M9W 6H8
Tel: (416) 675-2105
TLX: 06983574
FAX: (416) 675-2438

QUEBEC

†Intel Semiconductor of Canada, Ltd.
620 St. John Boulevard
Pointe Claire H9R 3K2
Tel: (514) 694-9130
TWX: 514-694-9134

†Sales and Service Office
*Field Application Location

DOMESTIC DISTRIBUTORS

ALABAMA

Arrow Electronics, Inc.
1015 Henderson Road
Huntsville 35816
Tel: (205) 837-6955

†Hamilton/Avnet Electronics
4940 Research Drive
Huntsville 35805
Tel: (205) 837-7210
TWX: 810-726-2162

Pioneer/Technologies Group Inc.
4825 University Square
Huntsville 35816
Tel: (205) 837-9300
TWX: 810-726-2197

ARIZONA

†Hamilton/Avnet Electronics
505 S. Madison Drive
Tempe 85281
Tel: (602) 968-1461
TWX: 910-950-0077

Kierulff Electronics, Inc.
4134 E. Wood Street
Phoenix 85040
Tel: (602) 437-0750
FAX: 602-252-9109

Wyle Distribution Group
17855 N. Black Canyon Highway
Phoenix 85023
Tel: (602) 866-2888
FAX: 602-866-6937

CALIFORNIA

Arrow Electronics, Inc.
19748 Dearborn Street
Chatsworth 91311
Tel: (818) 701-7500
FAX: 818-772-8930

Arrow Electronics, Inc.
9511 Ridgehaven Court
San Diego 92123
Tel: (619) 565-4800
FAX: 619-279-0862

†Arrow Electronics, Inc.
521 Weddell Drive
Sunnyvale 94089
Tel: (408) 745-6600
FAX: 408-743-4770

Arrow Electronics, Inc.
2961 Dow Avenue
Tustin 92680
Tel: (714) 838-5422
FAX: 714-838-4151

†Avnet Electronics
350 McCormick Avenue
Costa Mesa 92626
Tel: (714) 754-6051
FAX: 714-754-6007

Hamilton/Avnet Electronics
1175 Bordeaux Drive
Sunnyvale 94089
Tel: (408) 743-3300
FAX: 408-745-6679

†Hamilton/Avnet Electronics
4545 Viewridge Avenue
San Diego 92123
Tel: (619) 571-7500
FAX: 619-277-6136

†Hamilton/Avnet Electronics
9650 Desoto Ave.
Chatsworth 91311
Tel: (818) 700-1222, 6500
FAX: 818-700-6553

†Hamilton/Avnet Electronics
4103 Northgate Boulevard
Sacramento 95834
Tel: (916) 920-3150
FAX: 916-925-3478

†Hamilton/Avnet Electronics
3002 G Street
Ontario 91311
Tel: (714) 989-9411
FAX: 714-980-7129

†Hamilton/Avnet Electronics
10950 W. Washington Blvd.
Culver City 90230
Tel: (213) 558-2458
FAX: 213-558-2248

†Hamilton Electro Sales
3170 Pullman Street
Costa Mesa 92626
Tel: (714) 641-4150
FAX: 714-641-4122

CALIFORNIA (Cont'd.)

Kierulff Electronics, Inc.
10824 Hope Street
Cypress 90430
Tel: (714) 220-6300
FAX: 714-821-8420

†Kierulff Electronics, Inc.
1180 Murphy Avenue
San Jose 95131
Tel: (408) 971-2600
FAX: 408-947-3432

†Kierulff Electronics, Inc.
14242 Chamber Rd.
Tustin 92680
Tel: (714) 731-5711
FAX: 714-669-4235

†Kierulff Electronics, Inc.
9800 Variel St.
Chattsworth 91311
Tel: (213) 725-0325
FAX: 818-407-0803

Wyle Distribution Group
26677 W. Agoura Rd.
Calabasas 91302
Tel: (818) 880-9000
FAX: 818-880-5510

†Wyle Distribution Group
17872 Cowan Avenue
Irvine 92714
Tel: (714) 863-9953
FAX: 714-863-0473

Wyle Distribution Group
11151 Sun Center Drive
Rancho Cordova 95670
Tel: (916) 638-5282
FAX: 916-638-1491

†Wyle Distribution Group
9525 Chesapeake Drive
San Diego 92123
Tel: (619) 565-9171
TWX: 910-371-9592
FAX: 619-565-9171 ext. 274

†Wyle Distribution Group
3000 Bowers Avenue
Santa Clara 95051
Tel: (408) 727-2500
FAX: 408-727-5896

Wyle Military
18910 Teller Avenue
Irvine 92715
Tel: (714) 851-9958
TWX: 310-371-9127
FAX: 714-851-8366

Wyle Systems
7382 Lampson Avenue
Garden Grove 92641
Tel: (714) 891-1717
FAX: 714-895-9038

COLORADO

Arrow Electronics, Inc.
1390 S. Potomac Street
Suite 136
Aurora 80012
Tel: (303) 696-1111

†Hamilton/Avnet Electronics
8765 E. Orchard Road
Suite 708
Englewood 80111
Tel: (303) 740-1017
TWX: 910-935-0787

†Wyle Distribution Group
451 E. 124th Avenue
Thornton 80241
Tel: (303) 457-9953
TWX: 910-936-0770

CONNECTICUT

†Arrow Electronics, Inc.
12 Beaumont Road
Wallingford 06492
Tel: (203) 265-7741
TWX: 710-476-0162

Hamilton/Avnet Electronics
Commerce Industrial Park
Commerce Drive
Danbury 06810
Tel: (203) 797-2800
FAX: 203-797-2866

†Pioneer Northeast Electronics
112 Main Street
Norwalk 06851
Tel: (203) 853-1515
TWX: 710-468-3373

FLORIDA

†Arrow Electronics, Inc.
350 Fairway Drive
Deerfield Beach 33441
Tel: (305) 429-8200
TWX: 510-955-9456

Arrow Electronics, Inc.
1001 N.W. 62nd St., Ste. 108
Ft. Lauderdale 33309
Tel: (305) 475-4297
TWX: 510-955-9456

†Arrow Electronics, Inc.
1530 Bottlebrush N.E.
Palm Bay 32905
Tel: (305) 725-1480

†Hamilton/Avnet Electronics
6801 N.W. 15th Way
Ft. Lauderdale 33309
Tel: (305) 971-2900
TLX: 510-956-3097

Hamilton/Avnet Electronics
3245 Tech Drive North
St. Petersburg 33702
Tel: (813) 576-3930
TWX: 810-863-0374

Hamilton/Avnet Electronics
6947 University Boulevard
Winterpark 32792
Tel: (305) 628-3888
FAX: 305-628-3888 ext. 40

†Pioneer Electronics
337 N. Lake Blvd., Ste. 1000
Alta Monte Springs 32701
Tel: (305) 834-9090
TWX: 810-853-0284

Pionéer Electronics
674 S. Military Trail
Deerfield Beach 33442
Tel: (305) 428-8877
TWX: 510-955-9653

GEORGIA

†Arrow Electronics, Inc.
3155 Northwoods Parkway
Suite A
Norcross 30071
Tel: (404) 449-8252
FAX: 404-242-6827

Hamilton/Avnet Electronics
5825 D. Peachtree Corners East
Norcross 30092
Tel: (404) 447-7500
TWX: 810-766-0432

Pioneer Electronics
3100 F. Northwoods Place
Norcross 30071
Tel: (404) 448-1711
FAX: 404-446-8270

ILLINOIS

†Arrow Electronics, Inc.
2000 E. Alonquin Street
Schaumberg 60173
Tel: (312) 397-3440
FAX: 312-397-3550

†Hamilton/Avnet Electronics
1130 Thorndale Avenue
Bensenville 60106
Tel: (312) 860-7780
TWX: 910-227-0060

Kierulff Electronics, Inc.
1140 W. Thorndale
Itasca 60143
Tel: (312) 250-0500
FAX: 312-250-0916

MTI Systems Sales
1100 West Thorndale
Itasca 60143
Tel: (312) 773-2300

†Pioneer Electronics
1551 Carmen Drive
Elk Grove Village 60007
Tel: (312) 437-9680
TWX: 910-222-1834

INDIANA

†Arrow Electronics, Inc.
2495 Directors Row, Suite H
Indianapolis 46241
Tel: (317) 243-9353
TWX: 810-341-3119

INDIANA (Cont'd.)

Hamilton/Avnet Electronics
485 Gradle Drive
Carmel 46032
Tel: (317) 844-9333
FAX: 317-844-5921

†Pioneer Electronics
6408 Castleplace Drive
Indianapolis 46250
Tel: (317) 849-7300
TWX: 810-260-1794

KANSAS

†Hamilton/Avnet Electronics
9219 Quivera Road
Overland Park 66215
Tel: (913) 888-8900
FAX: 913-541-7951

Pioneer Electronics
10551 Lackman Rd.
Lenexa 66215
Tel: (913) 492-0500
FAX: 913-492-7832

KENTUCKY

Hamilton/Avnet Electronics
805-A Newtown Circle
Lexington 40511
Tel: (606) 259-1475
FAX: 606-252-3238

MARYLAND

Arrow Electronics, Inc.
8300 Guilford Road, Ste. H
Rivers Center
Columbia 21046
Tel: (301) 995-6002
TWX: 710-236-9005
FAX: 301-381-3854

†Hamilton/Avnet Electronics
6822 Oak Hall Lane
Columbia 21045
Tel: (301) 995-3500
FAX: 301-995-3593

†Mesa Technology Corp.
9720 Patuxent Woods Dr.
Columbia 21046
Tel: (301) 720-5020
TWX: 710-828-9702

†Pioneer Electronics
9100 Gaither Road
Gaithersburg 20877
Tel: (301) 921-0660
TWX: 710-828-0545

MASSACHUSETTS

†Arrow Electronics, Inc.
1 Arrow Drive
Woburn 01801
Tel: (617) 933-8130
TWX: 710-393-6770

†Hamilton/Avnet Electronics
10D Centennial Drive
Peabody 01960
Tel: (617) 532-3701
TWX: 710-393-0382

Kierulff Electronics, Inc.
13 Fortune Dr.
Billerica 01821
Tel: (617) 667-8331
TWX: 710-390-1449
FAX: 617-663-1754

Pioneer Northeast Electronics
44 Hartwell Avenue
Lexington 02173
Tel: (617) 861-9200
FAX: 617-863-1547

MICHIGAN

Arrow Electronics, Inc.
755 Phoenix Drive
Ann Arbor 48108
Tel: (313) 971-8220
FAX: 313-971-2633

†Hamilton/Avnet Electronics
32487 Schoolcraft Road
Livonia 48150
Tel: (313) 522-4700
TWX: 810-242-8775
FAX: 313-522-2624

Hamilton/Avnet Electronics
2215 29th Street S.E.
Space A5
Grand Rapids 49508
Tel: (616) 243-8805
TWX: 810-273-6921
FAX: 616-243-0028

MICHIGAN (Cont'd.)

Pioneer Electronics
4505 Broadmoor Ave. S.E.
Grand Rapids 49508
Tel: (616) 698-1800
FAX: 616-698-1831

†Pioneer Electronics
13485 Stamford
Livonia 48150
Tel: (313) 525-1800
TWX: 810-242-3271

MINNESOTA

†Arrow Electronics, Inc.
5230 W. 73rd Street
Edina 55435
Tel: (612) 830-1800
FAX: 612-830-1856

Hamilton/Avnet Electronics
12400 White Water Drive
Minnetonka 55343
Tel: (612) 932-0600
FAX: 612-932-0613

†Pioneer Electronics
10203 Bren Road East
Minnetonka 55343
Tel: (612) 935-5444
FAX: 612-935-1921

MISSOURI

†Arrow Electronics, Inc.
2380 Schuetz
St. Louis 63146
Tel: (314) 567-6888
FAX: 314-567-1164

†Hamilton/Avnet Electronics
13743 Shoreline Court East
Earth City 63045
Tel: (314) 344-1200
FAX: 314-291-8889

Kierulff Electronics, Inc.
11804 Borman Dr.
St. Louis 63146
Tel: (314) 997-4956
FAX: 314-567-0860

NEW HAMPSHIRE

†Arrow Electronics, Inc.
3 Perimeter Road
Manchester 03103
Tel: (603) 668-6968
FAX: 603-668-3484

Hamilton/Avnet Electronics
444 E. Industrial Drive
Manchester 03103
Tel: (603) 624-9400
FAX: 603-624-2402

NEW JERSEY

†Arrow Electronics, Inc.
6000 Lincoln Drive East
Marlton 08053
Tel: (609) 596-8000
FAX: 609-596-5632

†Arrow Electronics, Inc.
6 Century Drive
Parsipanny 07054
Tel: (201) 538-0900
FAX: 201-538-4962

†Hamilton/Avnet Electronics
1 Keystone Ave., Bldg. 36
Cherry Hill 08003
Tel: (609) 424-0110
TWX: 710-940-0262
FAX: 609-751-8624

†Hamilton/Avnet Electronics
10 Industrial
Fairfield 07006
Tel: (201) 575-3390
FAX: 201-575-5839

†Pioneer Northeast Electronics
45 Route 46
Pinebrook 07058
Tel: (201) 575-3510
FAX: 201-575-3454

†MTI Systems Sales
37 Kulick Rd.
Fairfield 07006
Tel: (201) 227-5552
FAX: 201-575-6336

DOMESTIC DISTRIBUTORS

NEW MEXICO

Alliance Electronics Inc.
11030 Cochiti S.E.
Albuquerque 87123
Tel: (505) 292-3360
FAX: 505-292-6537

Hamilton/Avnet Electronics
2524 Baylor Drive S.E.
Albuquerque 87106
Tel: (505) 765-1500
FAX: 505-243-1395

NEW YORK

Arrow Electronics, Inc.
25 Hub Drive
Melville 11747
Tel: (516) 694-6800
TWX: 510-224-6126
FAX: 516-391-1401

†Arrow Electronics, Inc.
3375 Brighton-Henrietta Townline Rd.
Rochester 14623
Tel: (716) 427-0300
FAX: 716-427-0735

Arrow Electronics, Inc.
20 Oser Avenue
Hauppauge 11788
Tel: (516) 231-1000
FAX: 516-231-1072

Hamilton/Avnet Electronics
2060 Townline Rd.
Rochester 14623
Tel: (716) 475-9130
FAX: 716-475-9119

†Hamilton/Avnet Electronics
103 Twin Oaks Drive
Syracuse 13206
Tel: (315) 437-2641
FAX: 315-432-0740

†Hamilton/Avnet Electronics
933 Motor Parkway
Hauppauge 11788
Tel: (516) 231-9800
FAX: 516-434-7426

†MTI Systems Sales
38 Harbor Park Drive
P.O. Box 271
Port Washington 11050
Tel: (516) 621-6200
Fax: 516-625-3039

†Pioneer Northeast Electronics
68 Corporate Dr.
Binghamton 13904
Tel: (607) 722-9300
FAX: 607-722-9562

†Pioneer Northeast Electronics
60 Crossway Park West
Woodbury, Long Island 11797
Tel: (516) 921-8700
TWX: 510-221-2184
FAX: 516-921-2143

†Pioneer Northeast Electronics
840 Fairport Park
Fairport 14450
Tel: (716) 381-7070
FAX: 716-381-5955

NORTH CAROLINA

†Arrow Electronics, Inc.
5240 Greens Dairy Road
Raleigh 27604
Tel: (919) 876-3132
FAX: 919-876-3132, ext. 200

†Hamilton/Avnet Electronics
3510 Spring Forest Drive
Raleigh 27609
Tel: (919) 878-0819
TWX: 510-928-1836

NORTH CAROLINA (Cont'd.)

Pioneer Electronics
9801 A-Southern Pine Blvd.
Charlotte 28217
Tel: (704) 527-8188
TWX: 810-621-0366

OHIO

Arrow Electronics, Inc.
7620 McEwen Road
Centerville 45459
Tel: (513) 435-5563
FAX: 513-435-2049

†Arrow Electronics, Inc.
6238 Cochran Road
Solon 44139
Tel: (216) 248-3990
FAX: 216-248-1106

Hamilton/Avnet Electronics
777 Brooksedge Blvd.
Westerville 43081
Tel: (614) 882-7004
FAX: 614-882-8650

†Hamilton/Avnet Electronics
954 Senate Drive
Dayton 45459
Tel: (513) 439-6700
FAX: 513-439-6711

†Hamilton/Avnet Electronics
30325 Bainbridge Rd., Bldg. A
Solon 44139
Tel: (216) 349-5100
FAX: 216-349-1894

†Pioneer Electronics
4433 Interpoint Blvd.
Dayton 45424
Tel: (513) 236-9900
FAX: 513-236-8133

†Pioneer Electronics
4800 E. 131st Street
Cleveland 44105
Tel: (216) 587-3600
TWX: 810-422-2211
FAX: 216-587-3906

OKLAHOMA

Arrow Electronics, Inc.
3158 S. 108 East Ave., Ste. 210
Tulsa 74146
Tel: (918) 665-7700
FAX: 918-665-7700

OREGON

†Almac Electronics Corp.
1885 N.W. 169th Place
Beaverton 97006
Tel: (503) 629-8090
FAX: 503-645-0611

†Hamilton/Avnet Electronics
6024 S.W. Jean Road
Bldg. C, Suite 10
Lake Oswego 97034
Tel: (503) 635-7848
FAX: 503-636-1327

Wyle Distribution Group
5250 N.E. Elam Young Parkway
Suite 600
Hillsboro 97124
Tel: (503) 640-6000
FAX: 503-640-5846

PENNSYLVANIA

Arrow Electronics, Inc.
650 Seco Road
Monroeville 15146
Tel: (412) 856-7000
FAX: 412-856-5777

Hamilton/Avnet Electronics
2800 Liberty Ave., Bldg. E
Pittsburgh 15222
Tel: (412) 281-4150
FAX: 412-281-8662

PENNSYLVANIA (Cont'd.)

Pioneer Electronics
259 Kappa Drive
Pittsburgh 15238
Tel: (412) 782-2300
TWX: 710-795-3122
FAX: 412-963-8255

†Pioneer Electronics
261 Gibralter Road
Horsham 19044
Tel: (215) 674-4000
TWX: 510-665-6778
FAX: 215-674-3107

TEXAS

†Arrow Electronics, Inc.
3220 Commander Drive
Carrollton 75006
Tel: (214) 380-6464
FAX: 214-248-7208

†Arrow Electronics, Inc.
10899 Kinghurst Dr.
Suite 100
Houston 77099
Tel: (713) 530-4700
FAX: 713-568-8518

†Arrow Electronics, Inc.
2227 W. Braker Lane
Austin 78758
Tel: (512) 835-4180
FAX: 512-832-9875

†Hamilton/Avnet Electronics
1807A W. Braker Lane
Austin 78758
Tel: (512) 837-8911
FAX: 512-339-6232

†Hamilton/Avnet Electronics
2111 W. Walnut Hill Lane
Irving 75038
Tel: (214) 550-6111
FAX: 214-550-6172

†Hamilton/Avnet Electronics
4850 Wright Road, Ste. 190
Stafford 77477
Tel: (713) 240-7733
FAX: 713-240-0582

Kierulff Electronics, Inc.
2010 Merritt Dr.
Garland 75040
Tel: (214) 840-0110
FAX: 214-278-0928

†Pioneer Electronics
1826-D Kramer Lane
Austin 78758
Tel: (512) 835-4000
FAX: 512-835-9829

†Pioneer Electronics
13710 Omega Road
Dallas 75244
Tel: (214) 386-7300
FAX: 214-490-6419

†Pioneer Electronics
5853 Point West Drive
Houston 77036
Tel: (713) 988-5555
FAX: 713-988-1732

UTAH

†Hamilton/Avnet Electronics
1585 West 2100 South
Salt Lake City 84119
Tel: (801) 972-2800
FAX: 801-974-9675

Kierulff Electronics, Inc.
1946 W. Parkway Blvd.
Salt Lake City 84119
Tel: (801) 973-6913
FAX: 801-972-0200

Wyle Distribution Group
1325 West 2200 South
Suite E
Salt Lake City 84119
Tel: (801) 974-9953
FAX: 801-972-2524

WASHINGTON

†Almac Electronics Corp.
14360 S.E. Eastgate Way
Bellevue 98007
Tel: (206) 643-9992
FAX: 206-643-9709

Arrow Electronics, Inc.
14320 N.E. 21st Street
Bellevue 98007
Tel: (206) 643-4800
FAX: 206-746-3740

Hamilton/Avnet Electronics
14212 N.E. 21st Street
Bellevue 98005
Tel: (206) 453-5874
FAX: 206-643-0086

Wyle Distribution Group
1750 132nd Ave., N.E.
Bellevue 98005
Tel: (206) 453-8300
FAX: 206-453-4071

WISCONSIN

†Arrow Electronics, Inc.
200 N. Patrick Blvd., Ste. 100
Brookfield 53005
Tel: (414) 792-0150
FAX: 414-792-0156

Hamilton/Avnet Electronics
2975 Moorland Road
New Berlin 53151
Tel: (414) 784-4510
FAX: 414-784-9509

Kierulff Electronics, Inc.
2238-E W. Bluemound Rd.
Waukesha 53186
Tel: (414) 784-8160
FAX: 414-784-0409

CANADA

ALBERTA

Hamilton/Avnet Electronics
2816 21st Street N.E.
Calgary T2E 6Z2
Tel: (403) 250-9380
FAX: 403-250-1591

Zentronics
6815 8th Street, N.E., Ste. 100
Calgary T2E 7H7
Tel: (403) 295-8838
FAX: 403-295-8714

BRITISH COLUMBIA

Hamilton/Avnet Electronics
2550 Boundary Rd., Ste. 115
Burnaby V5M 3Z3
Tel: (604) 437-6667
FAX: 604-437-4712

Zentronics
108-11400 Bridgeport Road
Richmond V6X 1T2
Tel: (604) 273-5575
FAX: 604-273-2413

MANITOBA

Zentronics
60-1313 Border Street
Winnipeg R3H 0X4
Tel: (204) 694-1957
FAX: 204-633-9255

ONTARIO

Arrow Electronics Inc.
1093 Meyerside Dr.
Unit 2
Mississauga LST 1M4
Tel: (416) 672-7769
FAX: 416-672-0489

Arrow Electronics Inc.
Nepean K2E 7W5
Tel: (613) 226-6903
FAX: 613-723-2018

†Hamilton/Avnet Electronics
6845 Rexwood Road
Units 3-5
Mississauga L4V 1R2
Tel: (416) 677-7432
FAX: 416-677-0940

Hamilton/Avnet Electronics
3688 Nashua Dr.
Units 9 and 10
Mississauga L4V 1M5
Tel: (416) 677-0484
FAX: 416-677-0627

†Hamilton/Avnet Electronics
190 Colonnade Road South
Nepean K2E 7J5
Tel: (613) 226-1700
FAX: 613-226-1184

†Zentronics
8Tilbury Court
Brampton L6T 3T4
Tel: (416) 451-9600
FAX: 416-451-8320

†Zentronics
155 Colonnade Road
Unit 17
Nepean K2E 7K1
Tel: (613) 226-8840
FAX: 613-226-6350

SASKATCHEWAN

Zentronics
173-1222 Alberta Avenue
Saskatoon S7K 1R4
Tel: (306) 955-2202, 2207
FAX: (306) 244-3731

QUEBEC

†Arrow Electronics Inc.
4050 Jean Talon Quest
Montreal H4P 1W1
Tel: (514) 735-5511
FAX: 514-341-4821

Arrow Electronics Inc.
909 Charest Blvd.
Quebec 61N 269
Tel: (418) 687-4231
FAX: 418-687-5348

Hamilton/Avnet Electronics
2795 Rue Halpern
St. Laurent H4S 1P8
Tel: (514) 335-1000
FAX: 514-335-2481

Zentronics
817 McCaffrey St.
St. Laurent H4T 1N4
Tel: (514) 737-9700
FAX: 514-737-5212

DOMESTIC SERVICE OFFICES

ALABAMA

Intel Corp.
5015 Bradford Drive, #2
Huntsville 35805
Tel: (205) 830-4010

ARIZONA

Intel Corp.
11225 N. 28th Dr.
Suite D-214
Phoenix 85029
Tel: (602) 869-4980

Intel Corp.
500 E. Fry Blvd., Suite M-15
Sierra Vista 85635
Tel: (602) 459-5010

ARKANSAS

Intel Corp.
P.O. Box 206
Ulm 72170
Tel: (501) 241-3264

CALIFORNIA

Intel Corp.
21515 Vanowen St.
Suite 116
Canoga Park 91303
Tel: (818) 704-8500

Intel Corp.
2250 E. Imperial Highway
Suite 218
El Segundo 90245
Tel: (213) 640-6040

Intel Corp.
1900 Prairie City Rd.
Folsom 95630-9597
Tel: (916) 351-6143

Intel Corp.
2000 E. 4th Street
Suite 110
Santa Ana 92705
Tel: (714) 835-5789
TWX: 910-595-2475

Intel Corp.
San Tomas 4
2700 San Tomas Expressway
Santa Clara 95051
Tel: (408) 986-8086

Intel Corp.
4350 Executive Drive
Suite 105
San Diego 92121
Tel: (619) 452-5880

COLORADO

Intel Corp.
650 South Cherry St.
Suite 915
Denver 80222
Tel: (303) 321-8086
TWX: 910-931-2289

CONNECTICUT

Intel Corp.
26 Mill Plain Road
Danbury 06811
Tel: (203) 748-3130
TWX: 710-456-1199

FLORIDA

Intel Corp.
1500 N.W. 62, Suite 104
Ft. Lauderdale 33309
Tel: (305) 771-0600
TWX: 510-956-9407

Intel Corp.
242 N. Westmonte Drive
Suite 105
Altamonte Springs 32714
Tel: (305) 869-5588

GEORGIA

Intel Corp.
3280 Pointe Parkway
Suite 200
Norcross 30092
Tel: (404) 449-0541

ILLINOIS

Intel Corp.
300 N. Martingale Rd.
Suite 300
Schaumburg 60194
Tel: (312) 310-5733

INDIANA

Intel Corp.
8777 Purdue Rd., #125
Indianapolis 46268
Tel: (317) 875-0623

KANSAS

Intel Corp.
8400 W. 110th Street
Suite 170
Overland Park 66210
Tel: (913) 345-2727

KENTUCKY

Intel Corp.
3525 Tatescreek Road, #51
Lexington 40502
Tel: (606) 272-6745

MARYLAND

Intel Corp.
5th Floor
7833 Walker Drive
Greenbelt 20770
Tel: (301) 441-1020

MASSACHUSETTS

Intel Corp.
Westford Corp. Center
3 Carlisle Road
Westford 01886
Tel: (617) 692-3222

MICHIGAN

Intel Corp.
7071 Orchard Lake Road
Suite 100
West Bloomfield 48322
Tel: (313) 851-8096

MISSOURI

Intel Corp.
4203 Earth City Expressway
Suite 143
Earth City 63045
Tel: (314) 291-2015

NEW JERSEY

Intel Corp.
385 Sylvan Avenue
Englewood Cliffs 07632
Tel: (201) 567-0821
TWX: 710-991-8593

Intel Corp.
Raritan Plaza III
Raritan Center
Edison 08817
Tel: (201) 225-3000

NORTH CAROLINA

Intel Corp
2306 W. Meadowview Road
Suite 206
Greensboro 27407
Tel: (919) 294-1541

Intel Corp.
2700 Wycliff Rd., Suite 102
Raleigh 27607
Tel: (919) 781-8022

OHIO

Intel Corp.
Chagrin-Brainard Bldg.
Suite 305
28001 Chagrin Boulevard
Cleveland 44122
Tel: (216) 464-6915
TWX: 810-427-9298

Intel Corp.
6500 Poe
Dayton 45414
Tel: (513) 890-5350

OREGON

Intel Corp.
15254 N.W. Greenbrier Parkway, Bldg. B
Beaverton 97006
Tel: (503) 645-8051
TWX: 910-467-8741

Intel Corp.
5200 N.E. Elam Young Parkway
Hillsboro 97123
Tel: (503) 681-8080

PENNSYLVANIA

Intel Corp.
201 Penn Center Boulevard
Suite 301 W
Pittsburgh 15235
Tel: (313) 354-1540

TEXAS

Intel Corp.
313 E. Anderson Lane
Suite 314
Austin 78752
Tel: (512) 454-3628
TWX: 910-874-1347

Intel Corp.
12300 Ford Road
Suite 380
Dallas 75234
Tel: (214) 241-8087
TWX: 910-860-5617

Intel Corp.
8815 Dyer St., Suite 225
El Paso 79904
Tel: (915) 751-0186

VIRGINIA

Intel Corp.
1504 Santa Rosa Rd.
Suite 108
Richmond 23288
Tel: (804) 282-5668

WASHINGTON

Intel Corp.
110 110th Avenue N.E.
Suite 510
Bellevue 98004
Tel: 1-800-468-3548
TWX: 910-443-3002

WISCONSIN

Intel Corp.
330 S. Executive Dr.
Suite 102
Brookfield 53005
Tel: (414) 784-8087

CANADA

Intel Semiconductor of Canada, Ltd
190 Attwell Drive, Suite 500
Rexdale, Ontario
Canada M9W 6H8
Tel: (416) 675-2105

Intel Semiconductor of Canada, Ltd.
620 St. John Blvd.
Pointe Claire, Quebec
Canada H9R 3K2
Tel: (514) 694-9130

Intel Semiconductor of Canada, Ltd.
2650 Queensview Drive
Suite 250
Ottawa, Ontario,
Canada K2B 8H6
Tel: (613) 829-9714

CUSTOMER TRAINING CENTERS

CALIFORNIA

2700 San Tomas Expressway
Santa Clara 95051
Tel: (408) 970-1700

ILLINOIS

300 N. Martingale, #300
Schaumburg 60173
Tel: (312) 310-5700

MASSACHUSETTS

3 Carlisle Road
Westford 01886
Tel: (617) 692-1000

MARYLAND

7833 Walker Dr., 4th Floor
Greenbelt 20770
Tel: (301) 220-3380

SYSTEMS ENGINEERING OFFICES

CALIFORNIA

2700 San Tomas Expressway
Santa Clara 95051
Tel: (408) 986-8086

ILLINOIS

300 N. Martingale, #300
Schaumburg 60173
Tel: (312) 310-8031

MASSACHUSETTS

3 Carlisle Road
Westford 01886
Tel: (617) 692-3222

NEW YORK

300 Motor Parkway
Hauppauge 11788
Tel: (516) 231-3300

EUROPEAN SALES OFFICES

DENMARK

Intel
Glentevej 61, 3rd Floor
2400 Copenhagen NV
Tel: (01) 19 80 33
TLX: 19567

FINLAND

Intel
Ruosilantie 2
00390 Helsinki 39
Tel: (0) 54 46 44
TLX: 123332

FRANCE

Intel
1, rue Edison-BP 303
78054 St Quentin-en-Yvelines Cedex
Tel: (1) 30 57 70 00
TLX: 699016

Intel
Immeuble BBC
4, Quai des Etroits
69005 Lyon
Tel: 78 42 40 89
TLX: 305153

WEST GERMANY

Intel*
Seidlstrasse 27
8000 Muenchen 2
Tel: (089) 5 38 90
TLX: 523177

Intel
Hohenzollern Strasse 5
3000 Hannover 1
Tel: (051) 1 34 40 81
TLX: 923625

Intel
Abraham Lincoln Strasse 16-18
6200 Wiesbaden
Tel: (061) 217 60 50
TLX: 4186183

Intel
Bruckstrasse 61
7012 Fellbach
Stuttgart
Tel: (071) 158 00 82
TLX: 7254826

ISRAEL

Intel*
Attidim Industrial Park
P.O. Box 43202
Tel Aviv 61430
Tel: (03) 49 80 80
TLX: 371215

ITALY

Intel*
Milanofiori Palazzo E
20090 Assago
Milano
Tel: (02) 824 40 71
TLX: 341286

NETHERLANDS

Intel*
Alexander Poort Building
Marten Meesweg 93
3068 AV Rotterdam
Tel: (010) 421 23 77
TLX: 22283

NORWAY

Intel
Hvamveien 4-P.O. Box 92
2013 Skjetten
Tel: (6) 842 420
TLX: 78018

SPAIN

Intel
Calle Zurbaran no. 28-1 lsq
28010 Madrid
Tel: (1) 410 40 04
TLX: 46880

SWEDEN

Intel*
Dalvagen 24
17136 Solna
Tel: (08) 734 01 00
TLX: 12261

SWITZERLAND

Intel*
Talackerstrasse 17
8065 Zurich
Tel: (01) 829 29 77
TLX: 57989

UNITED KINGDOM

Intel*
Pipers Way
Swindon, Wiltshire SN3 1RJ
Tel: (0793) 69 60 00
TLX: 444447

EUROPEAN DISTRIBUTORS/REPRESENTATIVES

AUSTRIA

Bacher Electronics GmbH
Rotenmuehlgasse 26
1120 Wien
Tel: (0222) 835 64 60
TLX: 131532

BELGIUM

Inelco Belgium S.A.
Av. des Croix de Guerre 94
1120 Bruxelles
Tel: (02) 216 01 60
TLX: 64475

DENMARK

ITT-Multikomponent A/S
Naverland 29
2600 Glostrup
Tel: (02) 45 66 45
TLX: 33355

FINLAND

OY Fintronic AB
Melkonkatu 24A
00210 Helsinki 21
Tel: (0) 692 60 22
TLX: 124224

FRANCE

Generim
Z.A. de Courtaboeuf
Av. de la Baltique-BP 88
91943 Les Ulis Cedex
Tel: (1) 69 07 78 78
TLX: 691700

Jermyn S.A.
73-79, rue des Solets
Silic 585
94663 Rungis Cedex
Tel: (1) 45 60 04 00
TLX: 260967

Metrologie
Tour d'Asnieres
4, av. Laurent-Cely
92606 Asnieres Cedex
Tel: (1) 47 90 62 40
TLX: 611448

Tekelec-Airtronic
Cite des Bruyeres
Rue Carle-Vernet - BP 2
92310 Sevres
Tel: (1) 45 34 75 35
TLX: 204552

WEST GERMANY

Electronic 2000 Vertriebs-AG
Stahlgruberring 12
8000 Muenchen 82
Tel: (089) 42 00 10
TLX: 522561

ITT Multikomponent GmbH
Bahnhofstrasse 44
7141 Moeglingen
Tel: (071) 41 48 79
TLX: 7264399

Jermyn GmbH
Im Dachsstueck 9
6250 Limburg
Tel: (064) 31 50 80
TLX: 415257-0

Metrologie GmbH
Meglingerstrasse 49
8000 Muenchen 71
Tel: (089) 78 04 20
TLX: 5213189

Proelectron Vertriebs GmbH
Max Planck Strasse 1-3
6072 Dreieich
Tel: (061) 03 30 43 43
TLX: 417972

IRELAND

Micro Marketing
Glenageary Office Park
Glenageary
Co Dublin
Tel: (1) 85 62 88
TLX: 31584

ISRAEL

Eastronics Ltd.
11 Rozanis Street
P.O. Box 39300
Tel Aviv 61392
Tel: (03) 47 51 51
TLX: 33638

ITALY

Intesi Corporation Italia S.A.
Milanofiori Palazzo E/5
20090 Assago
Milano
Tel: (02) 82 47 01
TLX: 311351

ITALY (Cont'd.)

Lasi Elettronica S.p.a.
Viale Fulvio Testi 126
20092 Cinisello Balsamo
Milano
Tel: (02) 244 00 12
TLX: 352040

NETHERLANDS

Koning en Hartman
Energieweg 1
2627 AP Delft
Tel: (015) 60 99 06
TLX: 38250

NORWAY

Nordisk Elektronik A/S
P.O. Box 122
Smedsvingen 4
1364 Hvalstad
Tel: (2) 84 62 10
TLX: 77546

PORTUGAL

Ditram
Av. M. Bombarda, 133-1 D
1000 Lisboa
Tel: (1) 54 53 13
TLX: 14182

SPAIN

ATD Electronica S.A.
Plaza Ciudad de Viena no. 6
28040 Madrid
Tel: (1) 234 40 00
TLX: 42477

ITT-SESA
Calle Miguel Angel no. 21-3
28010 Madrid
Tel: (1) 419 09 57
TLX: 27461

SWEDEN

Nordisk Elektronik A.B.
Huvudstagatan 1
P.O. Box 1409
17127 Solna
Tel: (8) 734 97 70
TLX: 10547

SWITZERLAND

Industrade A.G.
Hertistrasse 31
8304 Wallisellen
Tel: (01) 8 30 50 40
TLX: 56788

UNITED KINGDOM

Accent Electronic Components Ltd.
Jubilee House, Jubilee Way
Letchworth, Herts SG6 1QH
Tel: (0462) 68 66 66
TLX: 626923

Bytech Comway Ltd.
Unit 2 The Western Centre
Western Road
Bracknell
Berks RG12 1RW
Tel: (0344) 48 22 11
TLX: 848215

Jermyn
Vestry Estate
Otford Road
Sevenoaks
Kent TN14 5EU
Tel: (0732) 45 01 44
TLX: 95142

Rapid Silicon
Rapid House
Denmark St.
High Wycombe
Bucks HP11 2ER
Tel: (0494) 44 22 66
TLX: 837931

Rapid Systems
Rapid House
Denmark St.
High Wycombe
Bucks HP11 2ER
Tel: (0494) 45 02 44
TLX: 837931

YUGOSLAVIA

H.R. Microelectronics Corp.
2005 de la Cruz Blvd., Ste. 223
Santa Clara, CA 95050
U.S.A.
Tel: (408) 988-0286
TLX: 387452

INTERNATIONAL SALES OFFICES

AUSTRALIA

Intel Australia Pty. Ltd.*
Spectrum Building
200 Pacific Hwy., Level 6
Crows Nest, NSW, 2065
Tel: (2) 957-2744
TLX: 20097
FAX: (2) 923-2632

BRAZIL

Intel Semicondutores do Brasil LTDA
Av. Paulista, 1159-CJS 404/405
01311 - Sao Paulo - S.P.
Tel: 55-11-287-5899
TLX: 1153146
FAX: 55-11-212-7631

CHINA

Intel PRC Corporation
15/F, Office 1, Citic Bldg.
Jian Guo Men Wai Street
Beijing, PRC
Tel: (1) 500-4850
TLX: 22947 INTEL CN
FAX: (1) 500-2953

HONG KONG

Intel Semiconductor Ltd.*
1701-3 Connaught Centre
1 Connaught Road
Tel: (5) 844-4555
TWX: 63869 ISLHK HX
FAX: (5) 294-589

JAPAN

Intel Japan K.K.
5-6 Tokodai, Tsukuba-shi
Ibaraki, 300-26
Tel: 029747-8511
TLX: 3656-160
FAX: 029747-8450

Intel Japan K.K.*
Daiichi Mitsugi Bldg.
1-8889 Fuchu-cho
Fuchu-shi, Tokyo 183
Tel: 0423-60-7871
FAX: 0423-60-0315

Intel Japan K.K.*
Flower-Hill Shin-machi Bldg.
1-23-9 Shinmachi
Setagaya-ku, Tokyo 154
Tel: 03-426-2231
FAX: 03-427-7620

Intel Japan K.K.*
Bldg. Kumagaya
2-69 Hon-cho
Kumagaya-shi, Saitama 360
Tel: 0485-24-6871
FAX: 0485-24-7518

Intel Japan K.K.*
Mitsui-Seimei Musashi-kosugi Bldg.
915 Shinmaruko, Nakahara-ku
Kawasaki-shi, Kanagawa 211
Tel: 044-733-7011
FAX: 044-733-7010

JAPAN (Cont'd)

Intel Japan K.K.
Nihon Seimei Atsugi Bldg.
1-2-1 Asahi-machi
Atsugi-shi, Kanagawa 243
Tel: 0462-29-3731
FAX: 0462-29-3781

Intel Japan K.K.*
Ryokuchi-Eki Bldg.
2-4-1 Terauchi
Toyonaka-shi, Osaka 560
Tel: (06) 863-1091
FAX: 06-863-1084

Intel Japan K.K.
Shinmaru Bldg.
1-5-1 Marunouchi
Chiyoda-ku, Tokyo 100
Tel: 03-201-3621
FAX: 03-201-6850

Intel Japan K.K.
Tokai Bldg.
1-16-30 Meieki Minami
Nakamura-ku, Nagoya-shi
Aichi 450
Tel: 052-561-5181
FAX: 052-561-5317

KOREA

Intel Technology Asia Ltd.
Room 906, Singsong Bldg.
25-4, Yoido-Dong, Youngdeungpo-ku
Seoul 150
Tel: (2) 784-8186
TLX: 29312 INTELKO
FAX: (2) 784-8096

SINGAPORE

Intel Singapore Technology, Ltd.
101 Thomson Road #21-06
Goldhill Square
Singapore 1130
Tel: 250-7811
TLX: 39921 INTEL
FAX: 250-9256

TAIWAN

Intel Technology (Far East) Ltd.
Taiwan Branch
10/F., No. 205, Tun Hua N. Road
Taipei, R.O.C.
Tel: 886-2-716-9660
TLX: 13159 INTELTWN
FAX: 886-2-717-2455

INTERNATIONAL DISTRIBUTORS/REPRESENTATIVES

ARGENTINA

DAFSYS S.R.L.
Chacabuco, 90-4 PISO
1069-Buenos Aires
Tel: 54-1-334-1871
    54-1-34-7726
TLX: 25472

Reycom Electronica S.R.L.
Arcos 3631
1429-Buenos Aires
Tel: 54 (1) 701-4462/66
FAX: 54 (1) 11-1722
TLX: 22122

AUSTRALIA

Total Electronics
P.M.B. 250
9 Harker Street
Burwood, Victoria 3125
Tel: 61-3-288-4044
TLX: AA 31261

Total Electronics
P.O. Box 139
Artamon, N.S.W. 2064
Tel: 61-02-438-1855
TLX: 26297

BRAZIL

Elebra Microelectronica
R. Geraldo Flausino Gomes, 78
9 Andar
04575 - Sao Paulo - S.P.
Tel: 55-11-534-9522
TLX: 1154591 or 1154593BR
FAX: 55-11-534-9637

CHILE

DIN Instruments
Suecia 2323
Casilla 6055, Correo 22
Santiago
Tel: 56-2-225-8139
TLX: 440422 RUDY CZ

CHINA

Novel Precision Machinery Co., Ltd
Flat D, 20 Kingsford Ind. Bldg.
Phase 1, 26 Kwai Hei Street
N.T., Kowloon
Hong Kong
Tel: 852-0-223-222
TWX: 39114 JINMI HX
FAX: 852-0-261-602

CHINA (Cont'd)

Schmidt & Co. Ltd.
18/F Great Eagle Centre
23 Harbour Road
Wanchai, Hong Kong
Tel: 852-5-833-0222
TWX: 74766 SCHMC HX
FAX: 852-5-891-8754

INDIA

Micronic Devices
Arun Complex
No. 65 D.V.G. Road
Basavanagudi
Bangalore 560 004
Tel: 91-812-600-631
TLX: 0845-8332 MD BG IN

Micronic Devices
403, Gagan Deep
12, Rajendra Place
New Delhi 110 008
Tel: 91-58-97-71
TLX: 03163235 MDND IN

Micronic Devices
No. 516 5th Floor
Swastik Chambers
Sion, Chambray Road
Bombay 400 071
Tel: 91-52-39-63
TLX: 9531 171447 MDEV IN

JAPAN

Asahi Electronics Co. Ltd.
KMM Bldg. 2-14-1 Asano
Kokurakita-ku
Kitakyushu-shi 802
Tel: 093-511-6471
FAX: 093-551-7861

C. Itoh Techno-Science Co., Ltd.
C. Itoh Bldg., 2-5-1 Kita-Aoyama
Minato-ku, Tokyo 107
Tel: 03-497-4840
FAX: 03-497-4969

JAPAN (Cont'd)

Dia Semicon Systems, Inc.
Wacore 64, 1-37-8 Sangenjaya
Setagaya-ku, Tokyo 154
Tel: 03-487-0386
FAX: 03-487-8088

Okaya Koki
2-4-18 Sakae
Naka-ku, Nagoya-shi 460
Tel: 052-204-2911
FAX: 052-204-2901

Ryoyo Electro Corp.
Konwa Bldg.
1-12-22 Tsukiji
Chuo-ku, Tokyo 104
Tel: 03-546-5011
FAX: 03-546-5044

KOREA

J-Tek Corporation
6th Floor, Government Pension Bldg.
24-3 Yoido-Dong
Youngdeungpo-ku
Seoul 150
Tel: 82-2-782-8039
TLX: 25299 KODIGIT
FAX: 82-2-784-8391

Samsung Semiconductor &
Telecommunications Co., Ltd.
150, 2-KA, Tafpyung-ro, Chung-ku
Seoul 100
Tel: 82-2-751-3987
TLX: 27970 KORSST
FAX: 82-2-753-0967

MEXICO

Dicopel S.A.
Tochtli 368 Fracc. Ind. San Antonio
Azcapotzalco
C.P. 02760-Mexico, D.F.
Tel: 52-5-561-3211
TLX: 1773790 DICOME

NEW ZEALAND

Northrup Instruments & Systems Ltd.
459 Kyber Pass Road
P.O. Box 9464, Newmarket
Auckland 1
Tel: 64-9-501-219, 501-801
TLX: 21570 THERMAL

Northrup Instruments & Systems Ltd.
P.O. Box 2406
Wellington 856658
Tel: 64-4-856-658
TLX: NZ3380
FAX: 64-4-857276

SINGAPORE

Francotone Electronics Pte Ltd.
17 Harvey Road #04-01
Singapore 1336
Tel: 283-0888, 289-1618
TWX: 56541 FRELS
FAX: 2895327

SOUTH AFRICA

Electronic Building Elements, Pty. Ltd.
P.O. Box 4609
Pine Square, 18th Street
Hazelwood, Pretoria 0001
Tel: 27-12-469921
TLX: 3-227786 SA

TAIWAN

Mitac Corporation
No. 585, Ming Shen East Rd.
Taipei, R.O.C.
Tel: 886-2-501-8231
FAX: 886-2-501-4265

VENEZUELA

P. Benavides S.A.
Avilanes a Rio
Residencia Kamarata
Locales 4 AL 7
La Candelaria, Caracas
Tel: 58-2-571-0396
TLX: 28450
FAX: 58-2-572-3321